YOUR CHILD
AND THE PIANO

YOUR CHILD
AND THE PIANO

How to Enrich and Share in
Your Child's Musical Experience

by

Margaret Grant

NEW YORK   TORONTO

Cataloging in Publication Data

Grant, Margaret.
  Your Child and the Piano

ISBN 0-8253-0027-4

1. Piano – Instruction and study – Juvenile.
I. Title.

MT745.G72 1980   786.3'041   C80-094371-6

Cover design/Maureen Henderson

First published in 1980 in the United States by
Beaufort Books, Inc., New York

Printed in Canada   First Printing

ISBN 0-8253-0027-4

About the Author

Margaret Grant is one of Canada's best-known music teachers and adjudicators. Born in Stratford, Ontario, she studied under the Danish pianist Viggo Kihl and obtained her Licentiateship at the Toronto Conservatory of Music (now the Royal Conservatory). Joining the faculty of the Conservatory, she continued post-graduate studies and did considerable work as an accompanist and coach. She also studied with Claude Biggs, the English pianist.

Mrs. Grant has adjudicated at numerous music festivals, including five seasons at the Toronto Kiwanis, the largest music festival in the Commonwealth. She is one of Canada's most experienced music teachers, having taught piano in numerous Canadian cities. She recently conducted a seminar for the Ontario Registered Music Teachers' Association on problems of adjudicating. Her former students are in professional positions across Canada. A former member of the Council of the Ontario Registered Music Teachers' Association, Mrs. Grant presently teaches and resides in Toronto.

TO NORM

PREFACE

A new kind of parent has emerged in recent years. It is to this new generation of parents that I address this book. These parents would like to help their children to develop more fully their creative and intellectual gifts. They are anxious to be helpful but hardly know where to begin. I hope that much of this book will provide a fresh approach and that it will be of interest and value not only to parents but to students and teachers alike. Theirs is a joint venture; a difficult and delicate one.

The trend toward smaller families has caused parents to have greater expectations for their children. They are also aware of the increasing availability of excellent school music programs and want to encourage their children to be a part of them. Most parents are aware of the high cost of music tuition and the sacrifices that may be involved if lessons are begun. The marked difference in parents has been matched by an equally marked difference in the goals set for students. Once students had Carnegie Hall as their goal. Yet it was laughingly remarked that many young women got their music degree and then played the same set pieces for their husbands for the rest of their lives. Others "took piano" to a reasonably advanced level and now cannot play a note. What a waste! Now the goal is no longer the unrealistic one of Carnegie Hall. Instead it is the development of musicality as a whole. The likelihood of a child becoming a professional musician is small. However, it cannot be ruled out and still constitutes an important motivating force. Nothing is more unfortunate than to see an untapped talent or a door to pleasurable opportunity closed to a child forever. But the most compelling reason for studying music remains the personal pleasure that can be derived from this intimate and mysterious art form. Many people still find playing the piano a refuge from the strain of their daily responsibilities. And many others, having given up music study as children, wish they could.

The new goal that I should like to suggest for students is expressed best by the baseball term "triple threat". This concept embraces three different objectives: first, to play solos acceptably; second, to read at sight with ease and pleasure; and third, to be able to improvise, using a basic knowledge of keyboard harmony.

These objectives are more easily stated than achieved. Music study has always had a high dropout rate — 45% in the first three months and 90% after one year. Intelligent parents may admit that this triple threat concept is eminently desirable but just what moves must be made in order to have a sporting chance of success?

Perhaps you, as a parent, wish that you had started earlier to develop your own taste for the best in music. You will be encouraged by a comment in *Poteen*, a book by W. A. Deacon, a former literary editor of the Toronto *Globe and Mail*: "When a person comes to me to enquire what he should read to acquire a taste for the finest works of literary art, I always tell him to follow his nose. . . . The man must start with his own self-created instrument — the taste he then has. If he will read habitually what he likes, the chances are that his taste will swiftly improve, for the brain sickens of adulterated food just as the stomach does." The same thing applies to music.

Basically, I like to think of my book as providing a sort of liaison between parent and teacher. I hope that it will help parents to appreciate the difficulty a teacher faces in trying to touch all bases at each lesson in the limited time available. It should also help the parent to make the practice time more productive without destroying the initiative and sense of accomplishment of the child. (Not to mention the possible alienation of the teacher!)

There is a school of thought that contends that every student is different. Although this is certainly true, an astonishing similarity of problems emerges. To many, I offer no solution but, rather, a discussion of the pros and cons so that parents can come to their own conclusions.

Understanding what teachers are seeking to teach and what the essentials of good piano performance are is invaluable to the parent. Many onlookers at festivals find it puzzling and disturbing, for example, when a contestant who didn't make one mistake is beaten by another who, perhaps, having made some obvious slip, still emerges triumphant. Many intelligent people feel that piano playing is primarily a matter of reading the right note from the music, finding it on the piano, making sure to have the right finger, and that is that. From that point of view, it would be similar to painting by numbers, for many a fascinating pursuit. But you will see that having the right rhythm crops up as well. Unfortunately that is just the start. Having the right notes at the right time is merely a first step. Indeed, if nothing more were required, music could be taught very successfully by mail as it would be pretty much a routine process. There are a number of less well-known areas that make the difference between a good performance and a mediocre one.

For this reason, I have organized this book into two parts.

The first six chapters include practical advice on a wide variety of questions. The last seven chapters deal in more detail with the specifics of good piano performance. Although the last seven chapters are a bit more technical in nature, I do hope that interested parents will also read some of this advice. The task that the child is embarking on is a complex one, and parents can be very helpful if they are aware of the problems involved. Even better, perhaps a very interested parent will take a few lessons as well. They really are fun, if one doesn't take oneself too seriously!

The last chapters may also be useful to teachers looking for new ideas. As a teacher myself, I know how much one welcomes the chance to talk to other teachers and to exchange ideas. It is always heartening to know that others have had the same problems, have had trouble making decisions, and have had, at times, less than sensational results.

Table of Contents

Part One

Practical Advice to the Parent

1

BEGINNING THE MUSIC EXPERIENCE   3
Should Every Child Take Lessons?
"Stacking the Cards"
At What Age Should a Child Start Lessons?
Choosing a Music Teacher
Class Lessons
What if My Child Isn't Musical?
What Benefits Does One Derive from Music Study?

2

YOUR ATTITUDE TO THE CHILD   10
Two Ways to Make Practising Easier
Boys Are Different
Friends Can Help

xi

The Proper Attitude
When the Mother Works
The Mature Student

3

YOUR ATTITUDE TO THE TEACHER 19
How to Help the Teacher
Not All Pieces Need to Be Completed
Arranging and Paying for Lessons

4

COMPETITIONS AND EXAMINATIONS 26
When Should the Child Take an Exam?
Entering the Music Festival
The Difference Between Winning and Losing
Some Remedies for Nervousness

5

UNUSUAL STUDENTS 31
The Highly-Gifted Student
The Poorly Coordinated Student

6

DUETS 35
Some Keys to Success
Looking for Nuggets

Part Two

What It's All About:
The Specifics of Good Piano Performance

7

TECHNIQUE 41
What Is Technique?

The Choice of Good Music
How Technique Is Applied to Music
Learning to Play in All Keys — Blacks as Well as Whites
The Value of Slow Practice
Using Charts for Fun and Profit
Mastering Scales
The Star of Technique

8
TONE COLOUR   51
What Is Tone Colour?
Don't Be Too Critical
Balance Between the Parts
Soft Tones
Loud Tones
Pedal Exercises
Thinking Orchestrally
Choosing the Right Key

9
TEMPO   60
Speed and Comprehension
The Opinion of the Editor
Adjusting the Speed to the Student's Capacity
Counting Out Loud

10
CONSTRUCTION   66
Clues to Construction
The Importance of the Bass Line
The Deceptive Cadence
Use Modern Influences to Advantage

11
MEANING   73
Phrasing in Music
Sequences
Searching for New Ideas

12
SIGHT READING   78
The Uses of Sight Reading
Setting Up a Sight Reading Program
The Secret of Success — A Hymn Book
Adding Other Material
Learning Rhythmic Patterns
Winning the War Against Staleness

13
CONCLUDING NOTES   87
An Irreversible Urge

Part One

Practical Advice to the Parent

1

BEGINNING THE MUSIC EXPERIENCE

Should my child study the piano? When should a child start to study the piano? How does one choose a teacher? What benefits does a student derive from music study? It is not surprising that these questions recur. What is surprising is that, in spite of manuals that promise to make your marriage more meaningful, or that promise to make it easy to "think thin", there is nothing on the market to guide the parent with the problems of the musical child. Indeed, one sometimes wonders if there has been a conspiracy of silence in the music world, so rare are the published answers to these questions.

One of the most rewarding experiences that can come to parents is the delight of sharing an interest in music with their children. But this does not come by chance. Piano lessons are often a source of drudgery for the student and grudgingly endured by the parent. Johnny must be "given his chance". Sometimes a disappointing experience with a first child has been so devastating that the parents wonder, "Is it worth the aggravation to start another child? Shouldn't we just call it quits?"

The answer to that is a resounding "No!"

Should Every Child Take Lessons?

Let us suppose that you, as a parent, would like your child to study music. That, unfortunately, is not enough. I cannot say too strongly that, unless your child *wants* to take lessons, it is a mistake to embark on such a course. However, there is much that you can do to "stack the cards" so that he or she *will* want to. If your child is already begging for lessons, it is evident that you have already done some things right. Indeed, you may, if you care to, skip over to the end of the next section, although you may find some of it valuable in continuing to maintain your child's interest.

"Stacking the Cards"

It would be impossible to overestimate the value of creating an atmosphere suitable for the development of the child's interest in music from the day of birth. Competent observers now tell us that, from birth on, children have the capacity to differentiate sensations and demonstrate preferences. From the first days your baby is capable of learning. I suggest that, from the very first few weeks, some time be spent singing songs and reciting nursery rhymes to the infant. While the child is still a toddler, start playing records frequently. A wide variety of music, Broadway show tunes, light classics, jazz and rock music can be included with serious music. The selection need not be limited to Occidental music. Indian music, just like our own, has its classical and its popular idioms and parents with ethnic backgrounds would no doubt like to include music from their own heritage as well.

However, there should be discernment used. You must be vigilant about the quality of music played in your home. To allow a radio to blare all day long with commonplace music is to negate your other efforts. Buy arrangements made by musicians who are respected in their fields. As the child grows older, it is good for him to have some records of his own. So many children's records are available that is is impossible to give a list. You might keep in mind, however, hardy perennials like *Sparky's Magic Piano* and *Tubby the Tuba*. On the whole, it is wise to have nursery tunes on records sung by a high voice rather than by a baritone. It makes a more suitable pattern for childish voices to sing with. Many children sing at too low a range. Their best notes are around the C above middle C. Singing around the house, even if not of high quality, adds a certain radiance to the atmosphere. Two books that are fun to use are *The Baby's Opera*, published by Frederick Warne, London, now in paperback by Piccolo, and *The Golden Song Book*, published by Golden Press, New York.

After this stacking of the cards, it would be most surprising if a child did not desire lessons at least as soon as he starts to school. In the meantime, if you find that he is beating time or singing along with you, there is already an evidence of interest.

If you have not carried out such a program and your child shows no interest in music when he starts school, do not despair, it is never too late! You can start on a program, as of now, and still get pleasure from the enterprise as a family.

At What Age Should a Child Start Lessons?

Many children can learn to play the piano from the age of four. However, the small child has a short attention span and much of the lesson time must be spent in making the subject palatable. Better value comes from the purchase of first-rate records than on piano lessons at a very early age. A policy of having lots of music in the home makes for an optimum result when lessons do start.

Lessons with competent teachers are expensive, and, although children can certainly learn to play as early as four, little is lost by waiting until the child has been at a school long enough to know something of reading, numbers and taking direction. Although one hears many excellent performances by students of six, seven and eight at Festivals, late starters catch up quite readily.

One is wiser to start at age seven or eight with two half hours per week with a good teacher, than to start with "the girl next door" at an earlier period. Even a competent teacher is limited if the child is taking only one half hour per week. Sometimes a teacher will accept a child for a half hour but encourage the parent to supplement his effort. This sometimes works very well indeed especially if the parent and teacher are in rapport.

Choosing a Music Teacher

There is simply no easy way to pick a music teacher. Those who come highly recommended may not get along well with you or your child while another, whose talents you doubt at first, may prove to bring out the best in your child and you. Minimum qualifications should certainly include membership in a professional organization such as the Provincial Registered Music Teachers' Association. But, in addition to this, there are qualities of heart and mind that are determining factors in the success and ultimate enjoyment of your child.

The early period of study is crucial in establishing the emotional climate of the whole relationship. This is a more delicate matter for the parent than for the teacher. After all, the teacher has already had the experience of starting other students but for the parent, this may well be a "first".

In general I would say that the parents' attitude should be one of an interested observer who is willing to co-operate wholeheartedly if asked but who otherwise observes a hands-off stance. Parents who have studied to a reasonably advanced level won't find this easy but I assure you that it is a wise policy. An excellent relationship can be jeopardized by a tactless suggestion.

6

Class Lessons

Class lessons are now available in some areas, often in connection with the elementary school. There is no question that the facts of music can be taught effectively in classes and that the gregarious instinct makes for enthusiasm. However, although some unusually competent teachers get results for as long as two years, it is usually advisable to change to private lessons after the preliminary period is over and the child has learned the notes.

Class lessons can be helpful for the teaching of theory but *piano* lessons are a different matter. The piano presents complex problems not present in learning wind or stringed instruments. Five digits of different lengths and strengths must perform identically and, in addition, there must be a balance between the two hands. Bad habits are constantly erupting even with the best of teachers and eternal vigilance is the price of success. That is why I feel that an early change to a private teacher is desirable. One reason for the high drop-out rate in piano playing is the discouragement that results when having to correct bad habits ingrained from early years.

What If My Child Isn't Musical?

One of the commonest questions put by parents is, "If my child is not very musical, is there any point in studying?" As I have mentioned earlier, it is not desirable to have a child study unless he or she wishes to do so. Some parents feel that their child is lacking in musicality because of an inability to carry a tune, whereas many of the child's friends can do so. Such students are labelled "tone-deaf" and the parents resign themselves to the fact that music will have but a small part in their child's life. But this is usually an erroneous appraisal. Many school teachers make the same mistake. Dr. Frederick Staton, a well-known adjudicator who laid out the school music system both for

7

London, England, and for Australia, reached the conclusion after some research that only one child in 10,000 is tone deaf. It would be surprising if *your* child should happen to be the one in 10,000!

The problem is in "focusing" the voice — the same difficulty that one sometimes has with a camera. Rather than expect the child to sing songs, the parent should sing a single note, clearly, and have the youngster match it. A remarkable result is usually obtained in a very few weeks. The child will enjoy singing a note for you, the parent, to match. This can be great fun and in no time the child will be off to a good start for singing in elementary school.

Then again, many children turn out to be late bloomers and come into their own after what sometimes seems an unduly long time. So, even if your child shows little evidence of musicality, if he or she wants to start, by all means give it a chance. If your child continues to like it, there is obviously some value being derived from the work and it could very well add new dimensions to the child's life.

What Benefits Does One Derive from Music Study?

Music lessons are expensive: the one-to-one relationship is what makes them so. They can only be worth the investment if one obtains the maximum in benfits. One such benefit is in having a qualified person assess the student and help him to develop first-rate study methods. This improved learning technique is invaluable as it can be applied to the study of any subject. Music as a discipline has always been valued as a training for other professions. Dame Sybil Thorndyke and Miss Tanya Moiseiwitsch are only two of the outstanding artists in other fields who first started out to be musicians.

With today's crowded curriculum and so many demands on

8

the time of the student, it is essential that the best possible use be made of the time available. Added to this is the necessity of obtaining good marks to gain admission to desirable courses at university. That is why first-rate study methods pay off. Recently it was mentioned that 90% of the top 10% of students at both Oxford and Cambridge had been serious music students. An article in the *Saturday Review* on creative personalities noted that a surprising number of leaders in various professions were also competent musicians. In interviews these people said that they found music to be a catalyst in the sense that, while listening to music they thought of an idea from one discipline, wedded it to an idea from another field, and suddenly emerged with a brand new concept. Famous men who were excellent musicians include Paul Klee, the artist, who played for much of his life in the Berne Symphony Orchestra. Albert Schweitzer, despite his busy life as a doctor in Lamborene, added new insights into how Bach should be played; Albert Einstein, the famous scientist, had a life-long interest in the violin; and France's President Valéry Giscard d'Estaing reached a professional level as a performer.

Besides its value as a catalyst one other benefit emerges. Having to come up with a performance at a certain time whether one feels like it or not does develop confidence which is of tremendous value in a later professional life.

2

YOUR ATTITUDE TO THE CHILD

I have been a parent, a teacher and an adjudicator. Of the three, being a parent is the worst. The attitude of the parent to the child who has started music lessons is fraught with ambivalent feelings. At times things seem to be going well, the student is working very hard, yet the parent wonders if the child should be having more fun with other children. At other times, the same child will show a complete lack of interest or sense of responsibility making the parent wonder if the money spent on lessons isn't money down the drain. This chapter is drawn from my own experience as a parent and it has been a varied one.

I can recall, for instance, lying in bed early one morning listening to my small son practising Hanon's finger exercises downstairs. His standard was not just low, there *was* no standard. (It transpired that he was reading the adventures of Captain Marvel at the same time.) Frustrated, I found myself calling down in a cold weary voice, "Will you please come up and bring your book?" There was a long hallway leading to the bedroom and my son has since told me that trudging that long passage was like walking the last mile at San Quentin!

In spite of all the ups and downs, the pleasure one gets from a warm and satisfying musical environment far outweighs the inevitable moments of frustration. Each child is unique and one must face the fact that things will never be perfect. I am offering some comments that I hope will make it easier, and even fun, to traverse this tortuous path.

Two Ways to Make Practising Easier

It is unfair to expect a child to practise as soon as he comes home from school. Practising the piano is much more tiring than many people realize. Indeed, it is considered to be as heavy a task as doing a heavy washing by hand. To counter that problem, I have two suggestions to make.

First, choose a time when the child is rested and have some kind of food on the piano that can be eaten while practising to keep up the energy. Raisins, dried apricots or fruit juices are all suitable. It is wise to divide the practice time before and after breakfast. Some practice at noon means that the period at night can be free of obligation and, when used, can be a "fun time". A small child could start with three ten-minute periods each day. Children on that schedule have been known to ask permission to increase that to three *twelve*-minute periods. An hour a day for a young child gets excellent results and is a good mark to aim at. After the first year, an hour a day five days a week is the minimum that will make lessons economically feasible.

At a later date, with much more advanced work, longer practice is necessary. With high school students a real problem arises as to the best use of time with homework and other school activities so demanding. That is where considerable thought must be given to the matter of what should be dropped. No child can handle the myriad activities that are available to him, regardless of their value, and a ruthless cutting down must be done to ensure that the student has some free time in which to

11

do nothing, to browse or lie fallow. Many creative students have failed to live up to their potential because every minute was filled with "worthwhile" activities.

Secondly, children find practising lonesome. I am not suggesting that the parent *sit* with the child, but I do think it is helpful to be in the vicinity. Calling in suitable comments from time to time such as, "My, I'm sure that must be hard!" helps to spur on the child and gives a pleasant quality of give and take. It is frustrating to listen to a child playing aimlessly when you know that the work could be done more efficiently. But, in such a case, you must preserve a sense of values and consider that the ultimate goal is to maintain that irreversible urge toward music. It's part of the fun of music to tear through things letting the chips fly. You must avoid being so fussy that that joy is lost forever. My advice, on the whole, is to ignore such lapses. You can't put an old head on young shoulders and a young student simply doesn't have the same standard of excellence that he will have later. That is where a good teacher is helpful — he knows what is fair to expect and can hold up a target at which to aim.

I once encountered a situation that points up the difficulty of expecting adult standards from small children. Some years ago two ten-year-old boys wanted to enter the two-piano class of a local festival. After a great deal of work, they were able to negotiate the test piece but were lacking the grace and charm that was evident in the presentation of some of the more experienced entrants. Although the boys had been told that far better groups were competing, they soon began to be so fired with ambition that they pictured themselves winning. Indeed, they became so determined to win that they asked for the key to my studio and came each morning at seven a.m. to practise together. Although they managed to get the test-piece note perfect, it, of course, had the laboured and heavy-footed sound typical of ten-year-old, first-year-of-music boys. Bitterly regretting ever having consented to having them in the class, I appealed to their parents to soft-pedal any thought of winning. When I tried to take that line myself, the answer was always, "Well, they can't beat a perfect!" and "If we're perfect nobody can beat us!". They simply couldn't conceive that there was anything else to playing but the notes and the softs and louds. Happily, although they failed to place, they accepted the situation with equanimity. Indeed, when I sought them out to suggest that they buy themselves a treat on me, they were sunny and serene and quite untouched. That would not always be the case!

Boys Are Different

Parents must realize that at some stages of growth boys may become awkward and temporarily less well-coordinated. It is my experience that, although girls have some of the same problem, the boys have it to a much greater degree. Parents must avoid pushing qualities like grace and charm at this time. Sometimes the student finds that he hasn't retained his former speed and often there are inaccuracies and real difficulty in developing precision. This is a case where the new, larger hand just doesn't fit the piano. That will right itself shortly but, in the meantime, a great deal of encouragement is essential. Here is a place where the child's relationship with his father is often a determining factor. Some fathers develop a deep sensitivity to the frustrations of their sons and such interest and affection is invaluable in cementing a life-long shared interest.

Friends Can Help

Luckily boys and girls of this age, young teenagers, have a natural desire to be with their peer groups. Encourage your son or daughter to form a small group at school, possibly with friends who know no music. They will learn all kinds of skills such as helping the others to, say, sing arrangements that they have made themselves. Do not demand any kind of standard; it's the fun and experience that matters. Then, later at high school and university, your teenager will be able to have a part in more important musical activities that are exciting and enlivening.

The Proper Attitude

I realize that these comments on parental attitudes may have given the impression of just too much sweetness and light. On the contrary, I am well aware that, in the average home, some weeks are disorganized and nothing goes right. Parents are often preoccupied with matters far removed from music and often, as a consequence, extremely careless work — if any — is being done by the student. Few parents can resist making a caustic comment from time to time and I hasten to add it isn't too serious a matter as long as the general emotional climate of the home is one of warm affection. If you feel disgruntled, you may be sure the child will sense your dissatisfaction. It is extremely hard to hide your real feelings from a child. Even at a young age, a child will sense the displeasure you may be trying to hide.

On the whole, most parents are too critical of their children. This is particularly true of people who do not play themselves. They do not realize how hard it is to play things properly. People who do not know one note from another can still detect mistakes and mothers have to guard against calling in from the kitchen every time they hear a wrong note. That chill wind of criticism can wound a sensitive child and take away any pleasure that he or she might have had.

In general it is essential to have what I think of as a healthy fair-weather attitude toward music, one with no emotional storms. After all, when a child learns to ride a bike, falls are a part of the learning process. Cycling is also non-competitive: a child doesn't have to be the best rider in the block, merely a competent one. In spite of falling off many times, no one gets a nervous breakdown learning to ride and through this, a child

14

learns to attack a tough problem without loss of temper. By maintaining the same attitude toward music, the parent can help the child to experience the satisfaction of persistence and determination.

From my experience I would say that children should not work just to please their parents. I spoke to a neurologist friend of mine and asked him what policy parents should adopt toward their children's education. I felt that parents are sometimes overly ambitious for their children's success perhaps without too much regard for their health. My friend said that a student should have warm, friendly support from his parents but the student should definitely not work just to please them. It seems that we all develop goals by ourselves. If children gradually come to realize that their goal is unattainable, they will adjust it. However, if the parent keeps holding up the same old goal as a "must", *that* is what leads to breakdowns.

Your general attitude about your child's practising will have the greatest influence on the acceptance or rejection of practice. If you act as if it's an unpleasant task, a child will take the cue from you. But if you help in the right way, it can be made fascinating and stimulating.

The most musical child will balk at times. Teachers often note that the cleverest child is most difficult to teach. The youngster will go off at a tangent and always knows a better way. If your child doesn't want to practise, acknowledge these feelings, agree that he may not like to do it but try to get him reoriented. Do try to preserve your good humour. He needs your help! When a child is in a difficult mood, it is wise to have a heart-to-heart talk with him as to why things are going badly. We all know that a parent must be consistent in setting standards for acceptable behaviour. If you fail to enforce these standards, your child will sense that your rules are weak. But do temper the wind to the shorn lamb.

Start fresh! Without that credo, many of us would have gotten nowhere. When a child is doing badly, it is often helpful to get him to make a fresh schedule for himself. He needs lots of encouragement. Be frank with his teacher, but not critical, about the child's temporary lack of interest. Perhaps he could be given a new, easier but flashy piece that will get him into action again. Then he is on his way!

I cannot conclude these remarks without bringing to your attention one benefit that makes all the thought and care worthwhile. Music in the home is very often a factor in maintaining communications in the difficult teenage years. It is at this time that children often become unusually sensitive to any criticism. Parents are worried and deplore the fact that their children tell them nothing. A joint family interest in music, perhaps perfecting some ensemble work, lubricates the relationship and allows easy and relaxed conversation without the feeling that the parent is trying to pry into personal matters. As I have mentioned earlier, this should not be the sole prerogative of the mother. A show of genuine interest by the father heads off any of the now outmoded ideas that music has any sexist connotation.

When the Mother Works

In many if not most modern families the mother as well as the father works. I would be remiss if I gave the impression that mothers should always be home giving succour and support to their children, and that without this, the child has been in some way deprived. That is not the case. Although it is delightful if the parent has lots of free time in which to encourage the child, that is not always an advantage. No child should be the centre of the universe and a busy and active parent can provide the support that is needed even if the time is limited.

Some years ago, I asked Ann Casson Campbell, the daughter of Dame Sybil Thorndyke, what it was like to be the daughter of a famous actress who was constantly involved in her own work. Did she feel deprived? The answer was "No!" It seems that Dame Sybil had a certain effervescent affection that made the children feel delight in her accomplishments and privileged to be a part of her world. It is the *quality* of time spent with children that matters — not the *quantity*.

The Mature Student

With the mounting interest in adult education, many people consider renewing their interest in music and taking piano lessons. Some of these studied as children reaching varying degrees of competence. Others never had the chance to study and are fulfilling a dream that they have had for many years. To both of these groups I would say, "Do try it for a season!" There is much material that is available at every level and the student can find much to enjoy.

Seek out a teacher who is interested in keyboard harmony. Although it is evident that an adult beginner will not develop the manual dexterity that would be attained by someone starting early in life, there are still many avenues where the adult will actually have an advantage over the younger student. Mature students can have many hours of delight and interest by studying numbers within their range. They will also be surprised at their added pleasure in listening to music once they learn something of chord structures. They will, in short, have more of an idea as to just what it's all about.

Barry Tuckwell, the famous French horn virtuoso, told a master class that there are no secret shortcuts and there are no easy pieces. "I don't believe that horn players have 'off' days. They have 'on' days and they happen about twice a year!" Avoid taking your playing too seriously. Enjoy the taste of one chord going into the other!

One other point; after some years of *giving* direction, some find it hard to *take* direction easily. That shouldn't present a problem. Try to find someone who is essentially reasonable, non-authoritarian and likes teaching adults. You want someone who respects you for *your* expertise. Then there is a meeting of minds and there can be a delightful interplay.

Some of my best friends are former students!

3

YOUR ATTITUDE TO THE TEACHER

In discussing the relationship between parent and piano teacher, I should, at the outset, mention a few routine points that are important enough to bear repetition.

Before anything else, if your piano has not been tuned recently, have it tuned! It is easy to become used to a sagging pitch. Most people never tolerate for long a yowling radio or wobbly turntable, but too many parents are apt to be easy going about an untuned piano.

Once lessons have commenced, there should be no such thing as "missed lessons". The pattern should be the same as in school, that the child's only reason for absence is illness. "Not having had time to practise" is not an acceptable excuse for missing a lesson and indeed, in that case, the lesson is needed more than ever. If a good liaison exists between the parent and teacher, it would be wise for the parent to phone the teacher, and mention that little work has been done. Then the teacher will be able to take what steps are necessary to help the student to make the perennial fresh start.

On the whole, however, parents would be wise to keep a still tongue in their heads and resist the inclination to call about small matters. Naturally, in the first year or so of piano study, the teacher's time will be devoted to such matters as the facts of notation and the position of the hands, as well as the "fun" part of learning to play tunes by ear. It takes a great deal of time and effort before a new student can accurately prepare elementary work. But this time is well spent as it gives the student great confidence when he is able to work out the notation by himself. In spite of his passive role, the parent must let the teacher know that he is willing to help and support on request.

Few teachers stick to a rigid schedule and prefer the flexibility that is possible in the one-to-one relationship. They like to be able to take off on any subject, be it harmony, technique or whatever, when the student evinces special interest. Competent teachers have a goal in mind and know what constitutes logical progression toward that goal. In that way, any of the goals may be proceeded to depending on the response of the student.

No matter how competent the teacher, however, or how suitable the goal, all students run into what we call "plateaus". That is a period when progress ceases and the student seems to be stuck at that level. A first-class teacher is one who senses such a plateau before anyone else and, by a change of pace, inspires the student to pull out of it. With good teachers, one has almost a form of insurance that they will be alert to any lack of progress. They will discuss with the parent, if necessary, what can be done to remedy the situation, possibly even terminating the relationship if it seems advisable. This last possibility is discussed at more length at the conclusion of this chapter.

How to Help the Teacher

All teachers have the unpleasant task of competing with other interests for the student's time. The parent can help the student to decide which of all the "worthwhile activities" he or she will jettison. And there is another place where the parent can help. For example, most teachers realize the value of counting aloud but it is hard to convince a student of its necessity. Students usually say that they are counting to themselves. A helpful parent could laugh with the child about the difficulty of playing and counting at the same time and challenge them to count so loudly that they could be heard in the kitchen!

Those who constantly demand harder work forget that students need a great deal of preliminary material, of much the same level, so as to develop a facility and pleasure in sight reading and the confidence that accompanies such a skill. The principle of reinforcement comes in here and, as a parent, you have the chance to show amazement and delight at your child's growing ability to work through a piece without outside help. Here, the goal is the same as in general reading: if left alone in a house with books or magazines, one who reads for pleasure could have a fine time browsing. Similarly, if left alone with music and a piano, one who reads music easily could have an equally enjoyable time playing. That is why time spent developing this skill is rewarding.

Other facets of the work also take more time than one would suspect. For instance, we all realize that a gradual but steady crescendo — going from soft to loud — is an effective device. However, it is unfair to expect a relatively inexperienced student to do this. For first and second year students, it is enough to try for variety of tone in a less subtle fashion. For instance, one could try for an echo effect — that is, one part moderately loud and its counterpart played softly. Many teachers prefer to ignore *p* (soft) signs in the early stages and concentrate on helping their students to produce a clear bright tone with proper hand position. Playing softly requires much strength and ability. For instance, one's thumb can play more softly than the other fingers. As in speaking, it takes more trouble to whisper than to speak normally. (This is explored more fully in Chapter 8.) There are always many points that may not have been introduced by the teacher because, perhaps, the time was not opportune. All students have problem areas that beg for attention and yet one can confuse the issue by trying to solve too many problems at once.

Some years ago the famous soprano, Elizabeth Schwarzkopf, conducted a master class for singers. As each singer performed, it was evident that the rest of the class took note of various deficiencies and waited expectantly for her comments. At times so many things were wrong that it was hard to know just what would be remedied first. In each case only *one* item was chosen. For instance, Miss Schwarzkopf would say, "I think that I can help you with your German," and give specific help on that facet of the work. She was careful not to confuse the student by mentioning other problems that could not possibly be solved in the one session.

The late Ernest Hutcheson, famous Australian concert pianist and one-time President of the Julliard School of Music in New York, was asked what quality had led to his being so much in demand as a teacher. He replied that his secret was "Nose-to-the-Grindstone-itis". At each lesson he attacked one problem and spent what time was necessary to clear it up before starting on something else. He felt that many teachers try to cover so many points that few are really retained by the student.

Not All Pieces Need to be Completed

With the advanced student, the teacher is sometimes presented with an ambivalent problem of whether to drop a number that has fulfilled its usefulness or whether to try to get the number completed at the risk of boredom. There is the old moral concept that, once started, a project should be completed. Against that is the stock market adage, "Cut your losses". I incline toward the latter view. Indeed, it is often wise for the teacher to deliberately give students a physically demanding number that will broaden their horizon, but which will not be useful as a finished product for many years to come. This "stretching" walks a fine line between breaking the heart by work that is too difficult and providing the fun of tackling something exciting and stimulating. After all, students of literature study many plays that they would be unable to read intelligibly as actors.

Good communication or frankness between parent and teacher is essential here. Otherwise the parent might very well feel that the student "has been on that piece for a month and still can't play it!" Naturally, this physically demanding number is inappropriate for a music festival. The adjudicator can't give marks for bravery!

Arranging and Paying for Lessons

Most piano teachers think of a season as running from the first of September until the thirtieth of June, the same as the school year. (Students often take lessons during the summer months but that is arranged separately so as to fit vacation plans of both parties.) The ten-month period is divided into four periods, each called a term. The expectation is that when lessons begin in the Fall, the contract will go through until the end of June. Each term is nine or ten weeks in length and lessons at a conservatory are paid for in advance for each term. Missed lessons are charged for. However, if the teacher is notified 24 hours in advance, an effort will be made to make up the missed lesson at a mutually convenient time. The same is done with lessons that occur on a religious or statutory holiday. Private music teachers who are members of a professional organization usually follow similar rules. Although methods of payment can be varied, the policy regarding missed lessons is the same as at a conservatory.

Most students take two half-hour lessons each week but, as I have noted in Chapter 1, a few take one half hour per week.

When older, a student may take one hour per week as the attention span is longer and it saves the extra trip. The decision as to how much time is advisable can be made by consultation between the teacher and the parent.

It is considered unethical to make a change of fees during the season and, if a raise in fee is planned for the next season, the parents should be told of this ahead of time. This is so that they are not forced to accept a new fee structure because of lack of time to make another arrangement.

Although the parent owes the teacher a certain loyalty, the teacher also has responsibilities. Teachers are expected to have the student's interest at heart and to use the utmost discretion in regard to any personal matters that come to their attention. Here one expects the same confidentiality that is mandatory in other professional relationships. It is also their responsibility to get in touch with the parent if there appears to be a need to do so. Many companies have a rule among their executives — "No surprises" — that applies to this situation.

Many teachers feel that, if little or no progress is being made, the parent should be informed of this. However, many children who are not particularly musical benefit by lessons; it is part of their general education. If teachers taught only the extremely talented, there would be a dearth of well-informed audiences. From time to time, I have had students whose work was well below average and whose parents I informed of the situation. The parents had the feeling that the lessons should be continued despite the apparent lack of progress (in each case the child *wanted* to continue) and, in a number of cases, surprisingly good results were obtained in the end. There are always a few "late bloomers".

I hope that I have shown that the parent owes the teacher a great deal of loyalty and support even if that means, in many instances, remaining discreetly in the background. This loyalty must prevail even to the horrible moment when, after careful consideration, you no longer feel the sense of confidence that is essential. At that point you owe it to the teacher to discuss the situation frankly to see if there is still a chance of restoring mutual confidence. If not the teacher deserves acknowledgement of the work already accomplished and, only then, is it ethical to search out another teacher.

4

COMPETITIONS AND EXAMINATIONS

Once students have started lessons, the question arises as to whether or not they should try examinations each year and whether they should enter the local music festival. To a large extent the decision can be left to the teacher and the student. But, at times, the teacher consults the parents and wants their viewpoint before a commitment is made. There are students who thrive on a steady diet of exams and festivals and find that they provide incentives that encourage harder practice than otherwise might be done. There are other students for whom exams or competitions are just not the right thing. This has not necessarily anything to do with the child's gifts; it is just a difference in temperament. In the end, the student must make the choice. As I mentioned in Chapter 2, students should set their own goals and work for their own satisfaction, not to bring honour to their parents.

When Should the Child take an Exam?

One need not feel that students will do nothing if they are not trying an exam. We all have a certain "horror of mediocrity"

26

that gives us a natural desire to excel. Children change constantly; one year they will have no interest in an exam, whereas the following year they may want to try one. However, just because a neighbour's child tries an exam at the end of the first year is no reason for your child to do so. It is sometimes wiser to wait and consolidate the work. Children can pass an elementary exam without too high a standard of excellence. In my opinion, a good base is so desirable that the extra time that goes into perfecting detail is well spent.

At times the teacher may feel that extra time must be taken off the regular work in order to whip material for an examination into shape and may hesitate to do this. Many teachers feel that a spring exam is most desirable since much of the work has already been completed. When the exam is merely an incident in a long term plan, little time need be spent in special preparation. Then it is eminently desirable.

It should be noted that students need not try all the exams; they may try Grade 8 without having tried any others. But it is usually wise to try an occasional exam in order to "know the setup" and do well later in an exam of some importance.

Entering the Music Festival

If your child is going into the Festival, it is essential that you, as parents, do not take the matter too seriously. One can easily see that, in a large class and with a test piece of elementary level, it is quite possible for a large proportion of the students to play the number very well indeed; in fact, as far as the mechanics of piano playing go, many competitors may have it note-perfect.

But that, unfortunately, is just the beginning! Then there are the intangibles, things that are hard to put a finger on. One child will have a lovely warm quality of tone; another will have a certain indefinable grace and charm. How simple it would be if only one student were to have all those qualities, but that happens

27

only rarely! Though some qualities are necessarily more appealing to an adjudicator than others, a choice must be made. The situation is the same as if you were trying to choose a house; one has a gorgeous lot, but is too big; another has an appealing facade, but is too small; another has both surrounding spaciousness and a substantial look, but is too expensive. And so it goes. When the choice is between qualities like rhythm or good tone, it could go either way. That is why it is unwise to take the matter of winning or losing too seriously. (Naturally no one has worked hard for months without hoping to win.)

Here are some of the benefits of music festivals:

- A goal to work toward and a chance to be stimulated by hearing others performing the same number.

- A sense of camaraderie when the students run into each other in subsequent years.

- The lesson of having to perform at a certain time no matter what and of learning to meet deadlines.

- The sense of overcoming adversity successfully.

- The feeling of warmth and security of family support, win or lose.

- The value of having work judged, corrected and basic principles analyzed and made clear.

The important thing to note about all of the benefits listed above is that they can accrue to each student no matter what his or her achievement!

Nor do small slips necessarily mean disaster. Many adjudicators take little notice of small slips if the spirit of the music is good. With bigger mistakes, one can generally distinguish between forgiveable ones of nervousness and unforgiveable ones of carelessness. How a child recovers from a slip is often an indication of musicianship. Most adjudicators try to give each student a shot in the arm for next year. Adjudicators would be the first to admit that they could easily make a different choice tomorrow, or that a different judge might disagree. That is why the result is of small significance in comparison to the real values of the festival outlined above.

The Difference Between Winning and Losing

Given the benefits that can be derived from participation in a music festival it is important that parents not consider the matter of winning or losing too seriously. Nevertheless, it is natural for parents to ask, "Are there any ways by which my child can significantly improve his or her chances of winning?" The answer to this is, of course, yes. It is with this in mind that I have set out a number of chapters in Part 2 of this book dealing with the specifics of good piano performance. I have adjudicated at many music festivals and the elements discussed in these chapters have more often than not marked the difference between the successful winner and the also-rans.

Some Remedies for Nervousness

It might be wise to say a word about nervousness. Most students, even if they want to go into a test, find that they feel nervous and fear that they will do less than their best because of that. The parent may help by using a little amateur psychology. Explain to the student that we all know that when a cat sees its hereditary enemy the dog, its hair stands on end in preparation for flight. Humans, when fearful, feel certain physical changes to prepare *them* for flight.

Some of these symptoms are clamminess of the hands, knees knocking together, nausea and beads of perspiration on the forehead. Any or all of these symptoms are caused by the automatic rush of adrenalin into the blood stream. Although this rush gives added power, the disagreeable symptoms cause students to be

29

apprehensive as to how they will acquit themselves. They doubt their abilities. The solution to this is "Know thyself". One can learn to face the fact that those miserable feelings are the price paid for extra competence and speed. All the best performers suffer from nervousness. Their knowledge of physical makeup allows them to come up with a first-rate performance knowing that they have this added source of energy. As Katherine Cornell said, "I love rehearsals and preparation of a play but can hardly get myself onstage!"

The opportunity to measure oneself against the highest standards is as indispensable in music as elsewhere. But what can be an additional advantage is the warmth and friendliness that frequently pervades the atmosphere of a festival. When this climate exists, it galvanizes and inspires the weaker entrants as well as the strong. It is a determining factor in obtaining the best from each candidate. That is the reason many students look back on their festival experience—win or lose—as a highlight.

5

UNUSUAL STUDENTS

The Highly-Gifted Student

After a few years of study, it sometimes becomes evident that the student is more than usually gifted and the parents, naturally, wonder about the possibility of music as a career. Most musicians, no matter how much in love with music they may be, will agree that music as a hobby is unsurpassed but that, as a profession, it has limitations. It is not a field into which anyone should be directed. Only if students are determined themselves to pursue such a career, should it be considered.

There is a major difference between a performing career and an academic one. Certainly anyone considering a career as a performer would have to have shown extraordinary ability, usually at an early age. This could have been demonstrated by high marks in both Conservatory examinations and music festivals. But such high marks do not, by any means, ensure success on the concert stage. I do not propose to go into the matter of possible careers here but can say that there are increasing opportunities for those who wish to spend their lives in musical activities. In addition to the teaching of music in schools

31

and universities, there are posts for musicologists, librarians and critics. Universities often have "musicians in residence" and of course there are openings for both performers and commentators in both television and radio.

If your child should be gifted in the composing field, it is interesting to note that a new and lucrative use for his talents is in arranging and composing music for television and motion pictures. Many of our best composers are active in this area. It is not generally known that arrangers must be able to work in classical or contemporary music — Bach or Rock — with equal facility. However, anyone hoping to hold his own in this highly-competitive field needs the utmost in talent, skill and good luck to make it.

If the parent has reason to think that his child is unusually gifted, some steps are wise before too much time and money are invested. For this purpose I suggest that the "Seashore Measurement of Musical Ability" be used. These records, put out by RCA Victor in 1949, are not easily available but some music schools still have them.

They consist of a set of five records that are designed to assess the student in relation to the general population. It is like an I.Q. test in music. The records measure natural skills in recognizing differences in pitch, intensity, timbre and rhythm as well as measuring differences in tonal memory. For some years these records were used by the Eastman School of Music in Rochester as part of the admission tests. Similar aptitude tests could be devised by any music school. It is obvious that, if students rate highly in such tests, their natural capacities would be competitive with those of other professional musicians. If not, they should seek further advice as there will be a limit to how proficient they can be, no matter how much drive or ambition they may have. These tests, of course, leave out all kinds of extras such as personal magnetism that are factors in making a success.

Nonetheless, some students feel that they *must* be musicians no matter what the handicaps. Dame Edith Evans, the famous actress, felt that way about the stage. "The moment I was in the theatre, I knew that was where I belonged."

Referring to his early years in Russia, Peter Ustinov commented tongue-in-cheek that his parents begged him, in choosing a career, to be sure to choose something with safety and security like music and the theatre, *not* business or the law which were completely unpredictable. Here, until recently, parents have held the opposite view. That is why it pleases me to realize that a young person who chooses to make music a career can proceed toward a doctorate in that subject. It is encouraging to know that creative young people can choose such careers without feeling that they are gambling with their futures.

The Poorly Coordinated Student

There are teachers who feel that all students should play at recitals, try exams and enter festivals, as they provide necessary goals. I do not agree. There are many musical students who are poorly coordinated and who have no desire to be in a public performance of any kind.

No one gains by humiliation and no child should be put in a position of having to accept his or her own performance with shame or resignation. Some just haven't the hand-to-eye coordination or fine muscle control but these same students may be extremely musical and would benefit by a musical education. Some just can't develop the necessary strength, flexibility or agility and, if pushed into public performance, become confirmed in their own ineptitude.

Highly competitive situations are only suitable for certain types of people but there are many areas of music that can be explored with success and pleasure by non-competitive students. These possible areas include keyboard harmony and improvisation, to name only two. Choosing a teacher who will help the student to develop a good self-image will ensure that success is tasted in at least one of the fields that are open to the child.

6

DUETS

Duets at the piano are one of the most rewarding activities possible. They are such fun that they repay one for hours of lonesome practising. If you are one of the lucky parents who plays the piano — even if not too expertly — I do congratulate you. You will have many happy hours with your child. If you cannot play the piano you can encourage your child to invite friends in for duet playing and possibly offer cocoa and cookies as a bait in the early difficult days. Later, playing duets will be a self-propelling interest. At these get-togethers, the idea is not to learn one special number to use at a concert or at the local festival. Rather, the time should be spent playing dozens — even hundreds — of easy duets that can be handled with spirit, exuberance and just plain joy. There are many of these on the market but the ones by Diller-Quaile and Concord* come readily to mind. These are easy and can be done strictly for fun.

Now it may be that, at a later date, your child will want to play a duet at some public function and here is where I must

*See Diller-Quaile, *First Duet Book*, *Second Duet Book*, and *Third Duet Book* (G. Schirmer, New York); and the Concord Duet Books for First Sight Playing, based on Folk tunes: *First Duet Book (No. 608)*, and *Second Duet Book (No. 609)* (E. C. Schirmer Music Co., Boston).

ask you to lay down a very firm rule: if one player makes a mistake, as is usually the case, there must be no recrimination on the part of the other player or on the part of the parent. Any comment such as, "We would have won had it not been for your mistake" cannot be tolerated. The motto must be, "We sink or swim together!"

Some Keys to Success

Many areas, like tone colour and meaning, must be planned for in duets. I shall touch on just a few. The first thing to realize is that playing duets is like playing tennis. The ball, the melody, goes back and forth and the player must know just who has it from time to time. Obviously, if your child has the tune, it must be brought out, with the hope that the other part will be kept well under. Similarly, if *your* child has the accompaniment, he or she must take pleasure and satisfaction in keeping it properly submerged to allow the other part to take the lead. Sometimes this requires the rather difficult task of bringing out the bass and yet keeping the right-hand chords short and soft. Decisions must be made about expression — where the loudest part is and where the softest. Sometimes both students will be working up toward a climax, going very gradually from soft to loud.

Duets are excellent for the development of a really sharp eye for what should be brought out and what should be "thrown away". One must listen intently to make sure that, after the melody, the bass supplies a firm foundation. There is often a lovely counter-melody (one that in an orchestration might be suitable for a French horn) that must be given its share of the honours. At the foot of the list of priorities is the chord structure, whose only function, quite often, is to indicate the harmony and rhythmic pattern. This type of chordal accompaniment must often be subdued at all costs and sometimes that is very hard to do. Allowed to obtrude, it can be as objectionable as a buzz saw.

One can see why it is wise to play lots of easy duets so that one develops a hawkeye for spotting the marvellous opportunities that most people miss.

Looking for Nuggets

But now, what about the poor *secundo* player who rarely *gets* the ball. Both students should look for nuggets that will allow that player a momentary chance to shine. There are usually some effective bits that can be played with such distinction that the whole piece is transformed. I also suggest that students exchange parts so that they are used to the problems peculiar to both.

Occasionally, near the end of a number, both players have the tune at the same time. This is usually to suggest the idea that the two players are going along, arm in arm, with a really infectious swing, to a triumphant ending. Such a passage gives an opportunity for trim, neat meticulous work with the utmost in precision.

At the end, the hands of both students should be up exactly together. With both counting loudly at the practices, they will develop this style and precision. How different from some sloppy duet playing that we have all heard, where one could have made up a whole new piece from the rests that were ignored!

In more advanced duets, there is sometimes a fast part, *presto*, at the end. The students have to be extremely cautious and careful not to start at too fast a pace. That is where the habit of counting ahead for two bars and then swinging in is helpful. That leads to a lively vital start and yet not *too* fast. It is fatal if the team are unable to increase the speed for a brilliant finish.

Sometimes no one has the melody for the first four bars. In that case it is still wise to count ahead to ensure a good lilt to the rhythm. Then when the melody *does* come in, it is extremely effective.

Parents will be repaid many times for their effort in arranging these duet sessions. No, it is not easy at first. However, I assure you that the taste for playing with other people is one that leads to many warm friendships later, and to no end of stimulation. Indeed, the joy of playing together is why so many people are "hooked" on music.

Part Two

What it's All About:
The Specifics of Good
Piano Performance

7

TECHNIQUE

This chapter, and the five chapters that follow, focus primarily on what I consider the essentials of good piano performance. The ideas offered below are based on the experience of many of my music teacher colleagues as well as my own. Interested parents need not be concerned by the technical nature of this advice. Parents who have studied piano for a few years will find these chapters of particular interest, but even those with less musical background will find them helpful. Whenever your child starts taking piano lessons, it is useful to know something of the problems and complexities involved.

What is Technique?

Technique is not, as many people think, the ability to tear up and down the piano at the speed of light. Actually, it can be compared to the sharpness of a knife. Suppose that you have been asked to make some sandwiches for a special occasion. You know at the outset that you can't proceed without a well-sharpened knife. Technique in music is not dexterity but the ability to play a succession of beautiful notes. In brief, it is the ability to do what you want to do at the piano with a minimum of trouble.

When we as teachers refer to technique, we usually mean scales, chords, arpeggios, octaves and some finger exercises to round out the program. Our students often feel that the time spent on those areas could be better spent elsewhere. They feel that it would be more interesting to study additional pieces. Although there would appear to be some merit to this idea, it has been found to be erroneous. The bulk of piano music is deliberately designed so that it can be worked up in a minimum time by someone with facility in various technical areas. The same pieces, attempted by someone without that basic facility, would be impossible to master in months, even in years. A good example of this is the *Third Piano Concerto* of Beethoven, the one in C minor. In this, the first few bars of the piano part consist of nothing but the scale of C minor repeated three times, each time an octave above the preceding one. This would be quite impossible without an earlier developed expertise in scale playing.

The Choice of Good Music

Choosing suitable music requires more experience than a parent might realize. A good teacher will get suggestions from colleagues and will keep a record of pieces that work out particularly well and of composers that write dependable teaching pieces. Such composers write numbers that are "grateful" for the piano, since they work up well. At any student recital you will hear many of these. They are prized because they are attractive throughout and thus worth the time and effort expended.

Your child's teacher will try to avoid pieces that have knotty patches that cannot be mastered at that particular level and which mean that the piece must be abandoned and defeat admitted. Amateur dressmakers know that some patterns "make up" well whereas others defy one's best efforts. That is why home sewers continue to buy their patterns from companies known to be dependable. Similarly, your child's teacher will be using music from well-respected publishing houses since skilful editing will save much teaching time.

How Technique is Applied in Music

Most composers make a practice of using elements of technique such as finger exercises, scales, chords, arpeggios and octaves as their basic materials. When students have learned these basic segments well, they find that they can learn quite a difficult number in a surprisingly short time. Compositions can be broken down to their constituent parts and each of these mastered. Having already been able to negotiate the various technical figures with ease, all they need to do is to see what the pattern is and play it! On the contrary, if they cannot already handle the technical figures, no matter how intelligent they are, they will be unable to master such a composition even after months of work. Experienced teachers insist on standard fingering for the technical work because most composers expect this preparation.

At the time that George Gershwin wrote *Rhapsody in Blue* he realized that he lacked formal training in piano playing. In spite of this he had developed a formidable technique. He knew what effects he desired, but wanted, in addition, to ensure that his composition would be as playable as possible. So he asked Ernest Hutcheson, who became the president of the Julliard School of Music in New York, to revise it where necessary to make it more pianistic. This was done and we all know what pleasure that particular work has given many musicians.

Most technique acquired before the age of fourteen stays with one and needs little additional practice. Technique acquired after that must be constantly reinforced. That is why many good teachers feel that it is worth while to go to considerable trouble

43

to persuade a student to work hard on technique in the early years. Obviously, at the outset, few feel that the practice of technique is as interesting as, say, playing pieces. But as I shall try to show, many students can be sold, or inspired, to such a degree that they will do remarkably effective work in this area. That is why I think it is essential to push technique at the early stages as painlessly as possible. Below I have set out a number of ways to make it palatable.

Learning to Play in All Keys — Blacks as Well as Whites

Although it would appear to be "unfair to organized labour" to expect a young child to play in more than one key, much less in *all* the keys, I contend that it is not only feasible but that it is much more than worth trying. Not only does it not break the heart of the tiny tot, but it excites and thrills young children to feel that they are becoming as agile as a mountain goat, dashing hither and yon, up hill and down dale! Playing in all keys can be combined with ear training from the earliest lessons. With an easy tune like *Happy Birthday*, for example, the child can be shown how to play it by rote or imitation. G is a good note to start on:

This is in a suitable range for a young student to sing. When the youngster can do it easily, with any fingering, the teacher or parent may mention the fact that that could be too high or too low for some of the birthday party guests and suggest that he or she figure it out starting on C. Avoid being fussy either about fingering or about the inevitable long pauses. Soon the child will want to try starting on another note (say, D) and will have to do a little "monkeying around" in order to master it.

If by that time the tune is beginning to pall, the teacher or parent might be wise to experiment with some other simple tune — *Row Row Row Your Boat* comes to mind. Within a few months children following this suggestion are usually asking their parents to name a hard key to start on and managing to play a few little tunes that contain a number of black notes. In this enterprise, advice and encouragement are all that are needed because the interest becomes more or less self-propelled. Ferruccio Busoni, who delighted in creating difficult arrangements, feared that students might come to "think of the keyboard as a kind of gymnasium attached to a musical instrument." That problem is avoided when children learn to work out melodies in many different ways.

The principle is, of course, that we get tired of playing the same things. Playing any tune ten times in succession would turn off the most eager student, but trying to figure out something is in the same category as trying to work out a puzzle that catches our interest. Later, when the teacher presents the tones and semitones the child will have a head-start since he has already experimented with the black notes.

The Value of Slow Practice

Some years ago I asked a prominent teacher of ballet why the students of ballet had such superb figures whereas sometimes figure skaters, devoting equal time to a demanding discipline, developed hips that were — let's face it — too heavy. It seems that skaters needed to learn one of the secrets of ballet — the value of practising very slowly. We all know that muscle develops through use. The principle of just how this is done is simple — for a doctor of medicine. I do not propose to say more than that, after getting first-rate advice, skaters, like ballet

45

students before them, were encouraged to practise very slowly in order to develop the utmost in strength and flexibility. The result is that improved standard of grace and beauty of line that has had much to do with our excellent showing in international competitions.

For the piano student, the lesson is the same. Slow practice is golden. Indeed, I have often told students that practising a piece slowly is like putting ten cents into the bank. Playing the piece quickly is like taking out a dollar!

Using Charts for Fun and Profit

In the campaign to cajole the student into doing technical practice, I have found that the use of charts is tremendously valuable. With the parents showing enthusiasm, young students often become keen on practising technique and build up an amazing facility. The principle here is that a necessary part of good learning is to perceive and measure progress. It is best to arrange for small goals that are readily attainable to give the student a sense of accomplishment and the teacher a chance to show his approval.

The use of charts, made by the student himself with highly-coloured crayons, often provides the incentive to do some of the routine work that otherwise would be intolerable. Under the heading of routine work would be Schmitt exercises in all keys and in at least five different rhythms. This would only be assigned by a teacher after at least two years of study. Even the first page of Schmitt, ten exercises done in twelve keys and in five rhythms, makes six hundred individual exercises! Each takes about ten seconds to play and so, in all, that *could* require at least one hundred minutes of concentrated practice. A student completing a colourful homemade chart, in two weeks, gets much the same sense of satisfaction that an adult gets out of gradually completing a piece of needlepoint that would otherwise be boring. The student likes the respect that comes from having completed the charts. When students have had the responsibility of keeping up their own charts, they develop an objective attitude that permeates all their work.

Teachers may, of course, suggest charts for use by smaller children. These tiny tots love to make huge life-size charts all filled in to be taken to the teacher. But the assignment must be a small one so that a spectacular result can be obtained in minimum time. Such charts are great for the child who is embarking on the business of mastering triads. After showing him how to do C triad both solid and broken (the fingering *does* matter here) the teacher may enlist the parents' cooperation in encouraging the child to go further. For instance, after C has been mastered, hands separately, a child may then attack *some* of the white keys, then *all* the white keys. In the meantime, the child may try the key of C, hands *together*. This all takes a lot of doing and must not be rushed. Obviously the next step is to get all the white keys hands together and then attack the *black* ones, hands separately. Finally the child may now attempt another hurdle — the key of C, hands together, with closed eyes! Each of these stages will be broken into small steps so that the child is not overwhelmed. No new goal should be laid out until a certain satisfaction has been felt in the one already conquered.

This is, of course, the old principle of overlearning and leads to the fun of playing the triads in what I call "crazy ways". That could mean playing them in any odd way that the mind of man could invent. For instance, they could be done with the left hand playing solidly and the right hand broken. Then reverse. It can be even more demanding if one hand is played staccato and the other legato. Your child's teacher may have a group session for some of the students from time to time — a "class" — where youngsters are encouraged to play these for each other. Children love to think up difficult ways to play triads for their friends to try and a lot of laughing interplay results.

By the time students have learned all the triads, they really know the geography of the piano. They will have developed excellent technical prowess and can very much enjoy their powers. Technique should always be well beyond the grade of the pieces that are being attempted. A Grade Four technique for Grade One pieces makes for a delightful presentation. The result is a sense of joyous confidence that makes the whole performance a lively and happy occasion. Well worth a little work!

Mastering Scales

Scales present problems that tax the ingenuity of the best teacher who must be constantly vigilant regarding things like putting the thumb under. This is a difficult area and all I can say is that the teacher's enthusiasm and persistence are essential when this work is being initiated. In the end students should feel as if they were the pilots of a plane — sitting up there, supremely confident, surveying all their instruments, with ailerons in position, and so on. This corresponds to the sense of alert relaxation. The plane is literally running in oil and when the student is running in oil, this presupposes a complete lack of tension. Great skill is required from the teacher to develop this controlled relaxation. As they play their scales, such "pilots", then also observe their hands, especially the thumb, making sure that it is going *under* on schedule while going *outwards*, and coming *out* on schedule when coming *inwards*. Fun!

The teacher may stimulate facility in scale playing through an occasional "class" for scales alone. Boys and girls often become highly competitive when working on scales and love to pace each other. When they become more advanced, they work toward what I call "breaking the sound barrier". That is a very respectable speed: four hundred notes per minute. I might say that one rarely hears professional passage work, which includes scales, played at more than six hundred notes per minute, even on records. Beyond this speed, it seems, the human ear cannot distinguish individual notes easily.

In his book, *Playing the Piano for Pleasure*, Charles Cooke, best known for his sparkling articles in the *New Yorker*, speaks of the remarkable progress he made as an adult practising one hour a day. He says that when, as a boy, he studied the piano, he "enjoyed everything about it but the practising". Let's face it, piano practice is hard work and the main reason that most of us work on teachnique is for the satisfaction of keeping fit.

There are many ways to make this practice enjoyable but the natural tendency to backslide means that goals must constantly be renewed if peak efficiency is to be maintained. It is the teacher's privilege to present new goals and inspire the student to undertake them and the parent's to cheer the student on. It is wise, however, to acknowledge the student's distaste for this part of the work, and to help the child to be aware that no one always has things exactly as he or she wishes.

The Star of Technique

The teacher may take out a hard part of a piece for separate work. Cooke speaks of these hard parts as fractures that must be set. He says, "My approach to piano technique is perhaps unique, for I don't approach it with emphasis, or stress or insistence. I approach it with fanaticism, with mania. I practise special passages patiently, concentratedly, intelligently, relentlessly, until they have been battered down — knocked out, surmounted, dominated, conquered — until I have transformed them — thoroughly and permanently — from the weakest into the strongest passages in the piece!"

And here is where I want to speak of clock watchers. We are always given the impression that clock watching is bad. Not so! In some cases, it is really valuable. It is often inspiring for the more advanced student to think of how best to spend the thirty minutes per day that many teachers recommend for technique. I have found that my own students respond to "The Star of Technique".

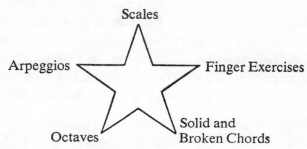

The teacher and the student together decide how many minutes to allocate to each point of the star. The decision might be made to spend seven minutes for scales, three for octaves, five for arpeggios, five for finger exercises, eight for solid and broken chords and the remaining two minutes for eating and drinking to keep up one's blood sugar!

Arthur Rubinstein, observing the number of young pianists with remarkably brilliant techniques, said, "We are raising a generation of soda-jerkers. The point is: what do they have to *say*?" With this in mind I have added a later chapter — Chapter 11 — on "meaning". Your child *will* be learning how to express his or her ideas musically.

8

TONE COLOUR

What is Tone Colour?

This is one of the most important parts of piano playing. It refers to the variation that one can get in the sound of the various notes to make the final presentation as effective as possible. Basically, the trick is to play so clearly that people can easily hear exactly what is going on. How maddening it is to be in a room with someone who is mumbling; you want to say to him, "Speak up, I can't hear you!"

In playing the piano the student is like an actor who must make more effort than he would in normal conversation and, indeed, often puts his arm out in a much more exaggerated fashion than he ordinarily would, to get his point across. He also shapes his words with care. We call that projecting and that is what a pianist must develop: a good clean, clear tone; a tone of distinction, like a Stradivarius violin.

It is good for piano players to think of themselves as painters, with the palette containing the primary colours: blue, red and yellow. Single notes can be considered as the primary colours and, just as in painting, a surprising variety can be obtained by

51

a little judicious mixing. Much of an artist's skill is in mixing these primary colours to get a complete range and they also show their ability in the way they use various intensities of the same colour. The young pianist wants to be able to play in a wider range than the ordinary,

The student's present range:
$$p \text{\textemdash\textemdash\textemdash\textemdash\textemdash\textemdash\textemdash} f$$

The range the student hopes to achieve:
$$ppp \text{\textemdash\textemdash\textemdash\textemdash\textemdash\textemdash\textemdash\textemdash\textemdash\textemdash\textemdash} fff$$

Don't Be Too Critical

Your child will be learning that harsh tones have their place. In some modern works there are what we call percussive effects where one actually hits the keys. Bartok and Stravinsky are only two of the composers who have repeatedly used such effects. Another familiar example is Prokofiev whose works include *Peter and the Wolf*. Encourage experimentation. A healthy clear tone is the primary objective but it can be made velvety too, if that is desirable.

Avoid being too critical of experiments. If your small child gives you a cookie with a grubby hand, are you not still pleased and grateful? The same is true when your child wants to play his or her own compositions for you. Nurture the idea. Do look for constructive things to say about them as they open one more avenue of communication.

Some years ago a number of experiments were conducted to see just what were some key motivating factors for children. A control group of six-year-olds were brought into a room that had been prearranged for the purpose. A number of articles were out of place — for instance, a broom was on the floor and a coat had fallen off a hanger. There were a few things to play with and, if the child ignored the disarray, something was said like,

"Why didn't you pick up that broom?" After the set period had passed, one of the leaders said, "Would you like to stay and play?" The children who were given even the mildest criticism stayed merely a minimum time whereas others who were not criticized, stayed on for a considerable time. That is, of course, just what we could have guessed but it does prove that if your child is willing to share his musical experiments with you, you should encourage this with the utmost warmth and affection. And you might encourage your child to play such inventions for the teacher.

Balance Between the Parts

When the young student has gained some control of tone colour, the teacher will begin to show how to make the piece more intelligible to the listener. By that I do not mean that every note must be made audible, not at all. I simply mean that the child must learn to allow the listener to taste the essence of the piece and get the meaning in only one hearing.

We all know how critical people are of an accompanist who drowns out the singer. We want to hear the tune and if it is buried beneath a noisy accompaniment, we are properly resentful. The young pianist faces this problem every day. From the very first year of lessons the students must be both singer and accompanist. To find out even more about this business of balance, I heartily recommend a hilarious recording made by Gerald Moore, one of the world's most famous accompanists. It is called *The Unashamed Accompanist*. This subject is touched upon earlier in Chapter 6, on Duets.

Basically, each piece has three components: the melody, the bass line and the accompanying chord. Most agree that the melody should be predominant. Then the next priority is the bass line. This is because it provides the structure that holds it all together. The purpose of the chord accompaniment is

53

merely to indicate what the harmony is and to enhance the rhythm. The idea of the harmony does not have to be overly stressed. Debussy has suggested that sometimes the accompaniment should be just like a whiff of perfume. The chords should be kept well under the melody and the bass line. Here, it is evident that the tone colour of each component must be controlled in relation to the other. The following is an example:

At the risk of overemphasizing, I want to say how difficult it is to keep these accompanying chords soft enough. Small chords played around the middle of the keyboard often come out more loudly than a single melody note that is some distance above the chord. It is expecting a great deal from a student, to keep those inessential chords properly subdued. It is everyone's problem. The most experienced performers still face this task of keeping the "nothing" material *under* and allowing the important areas to shine through. In speech we all know how boring it is to hear something reiterated that we already know perfectly well. That is why a student must learn to sift the wheat from the chaff and keep that chaff down. Sometimes it is helpful to make the insignificant chords slightly staccato and the melody legato. That allows the tune to sing through and helps to keep the chords in check. But it is a tough problem and never completely solved.

In Chapter 7 I spoke at some length of the value of practising triads. Here is a triad exercise combined with one for tone colour that will give you a practical example of a skill students must learn. This exercise and adaptations of it are worth the student's effort because they do much to solve the problem of keeping accompanying chords *sub voce*.

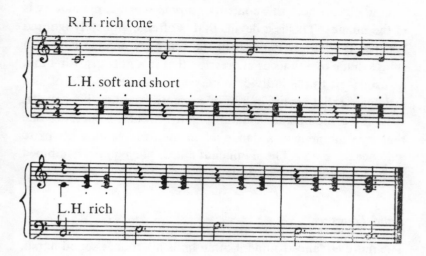

When your child can do this exercise easily, he or she has mastered a difficult aspect of playing. A surprising number of reasonably advanced students find such tone control difficult. It has been found that our inner ear hears what it *wants* to hear and not necessarily what is *actually* being produced. So the student must be encouraged to listen intently to make sure that he or she is really getting the result that is intended.

Soft Tones

When students have trouble obtaining variety of tone the teacher will spend additional time on the problem of obtaining a very, very soft *pianissimo*. It is difficult to make the sound both audible and full of conviction. In trying to play a note so softly players are tempted to relax and that of course, is the worst thing they can do. As in speech, it is more troublesome to whisper than to speak in a normal way, so in piano playing.

Oddly enough the thumb gives the best soft tone because it has the most control.

One place where this control of a *pianissimo* is mandatory is in the nuance. This is a device that is often completely ignored because it is rarely marked in the score. A nuance is such a subtle shade of colour or expression that it is not surprising that its use is left to the individual player. It can be thought of as a little pause that occurs in a lush, romantic number like a waltz. It is like a momentary catching of the breath, something like that rare moment in a dance when the tiniest pause seems to enhance the mood. The significant note is played *ppp*, combined with the almost imperceptible hesitation.

Loud Tones

The more advanced student often finds his chords sound harsh. This can be corrected by going into the keys more slowly. The quality of massive chords and even significant single notes is a complicated matter and necessitates the use of arm weight to get the rich warm tone that is so desirable. This is an area where personal tuition is required as it is hard to learn arm weight from any kind of text book.

Pedal Exercises

The pedal has not been considered and that is only because it comes into the picture after other preliminaries have been dealt with. A pianist who wants to produce the utmost in gorgeous tone should experiment with the pedal. One exercise that will give you a sense of what your child is learning is called "opening the piano". It helps to develop the radiance that comes from maximum resonance. This exercise is one I use to introduce students to the principle of syncopated pedalling and to get them used to the rich vibrant tone that can be obtained.

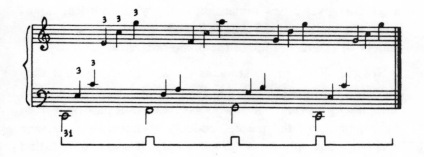

The first note is a full arm weight low C played by the braced third finger. This is braced by the thumb. The pedal is put down as soon as the note has been played. Then, still holding down the pedal, the student plays at random various votes of C chord with as rich a tone as possible and with maximum vibration. Then low F is played with the braced finger and as it is played the pedal is brought up. While holding the F, the pedal is depressed again and then random notes of F chord are played with the same rich tone. The same thing may be done with low G and its notes. Then a gorgeous, rich and velvety C concludes with the same Up Down pedal.

Thinking Orchestrally

Encourage your child to attend concerts and tell you what impressed him. Concerts given by orchestras, even amateur ones, serve a dual purpose. They nudge the student into considering the possibility of learning another instrument and becoming familiar with the various orchestral sounds. All piano students should be persuaded to learn a second instrument as it gives them a chance to play in groups with the consequent wider experience. The timbre of the various instruments becomes familiar and that is a source of pleasure later. What can be more exciting than going to a concert and sitting in the front seats to hear the characteristic sound of strings, woodwinds, horns and percussion? This gives a new dimension to the whole musical experience. Having tasted the unique sound of each instrument, the student will start to think of the piano orchestrally.

Not only must piano students *think* orchestrally, but they must learn to *play* orchestrally. For instance, consider a musician playing a French horn who has had a dull part right from the beginning of the piece. Suddenly a choice little passage comes up, but only for a very few bars. It seems only fitting that the other parts will allow themselves to be subdued in order to give this player a moment of glory. The piano student is like a one-man band, playing all the parts on the piano. The student is the one who must decide what parts to bring out and what to subdue. No doubt that lovely French horn part will be stressed so that the listener will really savour it. Similarly the student must learn to give his or her auditor the great pleasure of having some of these nuggets held up for examination. The reason that so many musicians are fond of Bach is that his piano pieces are full of charming spots that can be brought out in this way. Many students who discover such passages become Bach addicts. Such students have been given a priceless gift — a lifelong source of delight and satisfaction.

It is of value to hear such things as the standard piano concertos even if played by someone less skilled than a Horowitz. A first-class piece of music does not have to be played by the world's best artist in order to be beneficial. A good competent performance makes us familiar with the idiom and allows us to get more from a superb performance later.

Choosing the Right Key

Another aspect of Tone Colour that should be mentioned is the matter of range. It is often surprising to see how much more effective a song can be when sung by a singer having the suitable range. So, if your child is improvising or playing a melody by ear, you might suggest that he or she try it out in a number of keys to get the one that enhances the mood. Here is an experience that pointed that out to me. One evening I was the accompanist for a High School Music Night. I had the absurdly simple task of giving out the notes for each vocal part just before the boys' choir sang "Eternal Father Strong to Save". These notes were C, G, C, E. By some confusion with another title, I found myself giving out notes that were for another religious song — and were exactly a fourth lower. Just as I was playing the notes, I realized my error but it was too late to change. I felt that I had no alternative but to say nothing. So the boys proceeded, with muttered prayers from me that they would be able to hit the low notes.

After the concert, still not having admitted my mistake, I ran into a very competent musician, the teacher of music in another school. He had been quite taken by the concert but said that its high note (!) was the singing of the boys' choir. He had never heard them sound so rich and mellow! The end of this story is that later, when we were discussing suitable entries for the Toronto Music Festival, I suggested that the boys' choir sing their "Eternal Father" at a much lower pitch for added resonance! They won the class!

9

TEMPO

Choosing a suitable tempo has always been a problem and many of our best musicians have widely varying views. One has only to time a number of recordings of the same number to see that this is so. If you timed the Tchaikovsky *Concerto in B flat* played by Arthur Rubinstein and also by Van Cliburn, there would be a marked difference in total time. If Rubinstein took 37 minutes and Van Cliburn managed to whip through it in 28 minutes, does that mean that Cliburn is the better pianist? These figures might well be reversed in new recordings by the same pianists.

Hans Richter, the famous conductor of the turn of the century, said, "If it sounds fast, it's too fast, and if it sounds slow, it's too slow." That seems to be ridiculous but, on second thought, it says it all! The big thing is: if the tempo enhances the mood, it is right; if it destroys the mood, it's wrong.

In many compositions the performer is like a lawyer presenting a case and trying to make it convincing. A lawyer chooses to speak at a speed that will add conviction to the presentation.

Speed and Comprehension

There is a modern tendency to play too quickly. There are now such excellent methods of teaching piano technique that there are many very fine pianists who can negotiate the most difficult passages with ease. Indeed, often, if the speed is too great, a number can sound just as incomprehensible as a tape running backwards. Helen Hayes recounts that, when preparing *The Cherry Orchard* of Chekhov, the director finally said, "That is a superb production, but we'll have to cut off eight minutes because it's for television." So the actors slightly increased the pace in order to comply with the director's wish. When they saw it on television they found it meaningless!

A counter example can be found in the Duo Art recordings that were made on piano rolls many years ago by famous pianists like Hofmann and Paderewski. These recordings were discontinued when it was found that it was impossible to duplicate the true intensity of tone. However, on these player-piano-like rolls, we can hear exactly the speed at which these artists played. In all cases, the speed was much less than present-day recordings. With so many recording devices, the public has become familiar with these compositions and would be bored at hearing them played more slowly.

Everyone takes it for granted that, in an area like marches, there would be little argument. Wrong! At a marching-band competition in Florida a few years ago, I clocked marchers at all speeds between 92 and 144 steps per minute. Groups like the solid Highlanders chose a sensible, sound pace and did not deviate from that. Exuberant High School bands with a high proportion of young students often were positively prancing, at the highest speed. We all have a natural rhythm that suits us and that is true not only of walking but of speech. Our speech, of course, is variable, but can usually be easily recognized by our friends.

The Opinion of the Editor

When the student begins to tackle the problem of speed, he or she becomes something of a detective looking for clues. The first clue is the metronome marking at the top of the page, put in, usually, by the editor. It is wise to buy music from a respected publisher (any music store can advise you on this) because, for the price you pay, you get a good editor's comments. However, even when one has a good editor, opinions are still open to question.

Many years ago the Winnipeg Music Festival had the famous Bach specialist, Harold Samuels, as adjudicator. His fame was such that, were he to announce a series of five all-Bach concerts, they would be a sellout at once. To take advantage of his presence, I prepared as many Bach entries as possible with the very few students I had at that time. The test piece was the first section of one of the Bach Partitas and there were about twenty entrants. The Schirmer edition, which was listed in the Festival syllabus, suggested a Metronome speed of one quarter note to 100 (100 quarter notes per minute).

Most of the students, including my own entry, found that that speed was very difficult indeed, but still negotiable. You can imagine our surprise and chagrin when we found that the eventual winners of the class had all played it much more slowly. The teachers, of course, were furious and, in conversation among themselves expressed considerable dissatisfaction with the whole affair. Being one of the younger teachers, I suggested that someone ask Mr. Samuels about it. That seemed to be a completely ridiculous idea and one not worth serious consideration. The matter continued to nag at my mind until, on one occasion, when I found myself alone with Mr. Samuels, I decided to take a chance and broach the subject.

My heart was beating at a very high rate but I still remember that I said something like this: "Mr. Samuels, I wonder if I could ask you a question about the Bach Partita class. You don't know which one was my student and I am not complaining. However, I couldn't help noticing that, although the edition suggested a speed of 100-1, the winners were all ones who had played it at less than half that figure." He was very angry and insulted that anyone should question his judgment. His answer was, "Well, of course it boils down to whose opinion you value most — mine or the editors?" I have rarely been more upset but by now being into it, I pulled myself together. "In my case," I said, "it wasn't a matter of choosing the editor rather than you — it was a case of did I value *my* opinion more than that of the editor." He saw my point and, completely changing his stance, told me in a very friendly fashion how variable are editors' opinions.

Since then, I have tried to consider carefully an editor's viewpoint but, if it proved to be unsuitable for my student, I have changed it without a qualm. Indeed, in many cases even if one agrees with the editor's choice of tempo, it may still not be suitable for the particular student who is working on that number. The student may not be capable of handling it at the speed indicated.

Adjusting the Speed to the Student's Capacity

At a festival some years ago, I had one entrant who could handle the test piece beautifully at a slow pace but who simply hadn't the control necessary to play it at the Metronome speed marked: 100-1 (100 quarter notes per minute). This was not a matter of preference. We both realized that the number would be more effective at a fast pace but my student was quite unable to bring it off at her present stage of technique. So she performed at the speed that she *could* manage and, although she did well, was not surprised to hear the adjudicator say, "You managed so many other details, did you not see that the speed was marked at

100-1?" As you can see, the decisions the teacher and student must make are not easy!

Sometimes students will buy a record of their piece played by someone like Horowitz, who dashes along with his usual breathtaking lightness and grace. Here again, choices must be made: Horowitz, with his high performance engine, can do anything; the student, with a Volkswagen engine, must live with built-in limitations. The teacher, of course, will try to get the utmost in the way of perfection of detail at the lower speed. This can make for a very acceptable and musical performance.

A case comes to mind. In a two-piano class there were a number of entrants and extremely keen competition between my students and some teams put in by another teacher — a very warm friend. She told me, laughingly, that she had learned at what speed my team would be playing the test piece — a Moskowski Spanish Dance. Her students, in an effort to leave no stone unturned had gone to my studio at 7 a.m. and clocked my team who were practising. My colleague and I were highly amused at this but I was well aware that my two girls, although very musical, had never done enough plain honest work to attain the slick technique necessary. They just didn't have the precision, style and grace of one of their competitors. So, just for fun, with a little guile mixed in, I changed the speed of my pair. We completely changed our interpretation and they played at the slowest possible pace with emotion dripping all over the place. No, they didn't win, but the adjudicator remarked, "What a pleasant change."

In a festival the teacher may decide that the test piece should go as quickly as possible. Then it is like a relay race. If the student goes too quickly, there is the danger of disaster and of the whole thing being thrown away. On the other hand, if the student plays cautiously, there is a chance that someone more daring will win. The final decision is a delicate one with little to do with musicality and much to do with the teacher's estimate of the student's strengths. The main thing is to find the most comfortable speed. We all know that a student would rather wear a pair of jeans that are the right length than an impeccable pair of trousers of a length that makes one feel self-conscious.

Counting Out Loud

In professional life rehearsals have become so expensive that groups are lucky to have even one rehearsal before a performance. That is why students are urged to count aloud constantly as a habit. It prevents the practice of playing easy parts more quickly than hard parts and it is impossible to overestimate its value. I know of no professional musician who does not count. The famous comedian, Danny Kaye, made it his practice to count in the wings before he flew in to start one of his songs. His habit of counting two bars ahead, and then swinging in, is one that I most heartily recommend.

In closing, I think that students might be encouraged to observe the tempi chosen by fine artists at concerts. An easy way to clock a performer is to use a watch with an easily readable second hand. The student should get a feeling for the beat and then see how many beats are contained in a twelve second interval. Multiplying this by five will give the applicable metronome speed. Minuets vary from eighty-four to one hundred and forty-four!

We tend to think that it is easy to play slowly but such is not the case. Witness Ashkenazy playing an Adagio at 36 beats per minute. It would be hard to walk at that inordinately slow pace. Try it! Only a virtuoso can play so slowly and still make the composition viable!

10

CONSTRUCTION

Construction in music is exactly the same as it is in any other field. In architecture, it is the basic plan by which the building is erected, with bearing walls in certain places, decorative facing in other areas. In literature, it is the story's plot, perhaps the old favorite: boy meets girl, boy loses girl, boy regains girl. A knowledge of the plan is as essential in music as in literature. The best compositions, even very short ones such as Mozart's *Minuet in F*, written when he was only six years of age, have a sense of continuity, of one step leading to another, of details fitting gradually into a larger design.

To get the sense of construction of a number, the teacher may show the student how to play through the stark skeleton of the piece using just the basic chords. Usually one finds the boldest and most striking chords toward the end.

We all know that we remember best when there is a pattern. However, sophisticated listeners become bored if the pattern is too obvious or too often repeated. For instance, in some music in the popular field the harmony is of such an elementary nature that listening to it is something like reading a primer. There is nothing *wrong* with it; it is simply lacking in interest. On the

66

other hand, well-known melodies that have become tiresome through familiarity, can be transformed by the addition of interesting and inventive counterpoint. When the basic harmony is freshened up as well, the result is a number that appeals to those who know the tune, recognize it and like it, and to those who find the new treatment intriguing.

Richard R. Bennett, whose connection with the Broadway show-tune field is legendary, has said that the whole difference in such material is in the originality of the counterpoint. One has only to listen to the sound track of a Fred Astaire movie to realize the truth of this. All those swirling runs and arpeggios give an opulence to the whole that is exciting. A simpler example is that of a Sousa March — *The Stars and Stripes Forever* — with its well-known sparkling counter tunes played by the piccolos in the final peroration.

Clues to Construction

Appreciation of the construction increases with knowledge of elementary harmony but one can still get a fair idea through plain common sense. The trick is to watch for a clue here and a clue there. For instance, the first 8 bars (a musical sentence) could be in a major key sounding reasonably forthright and sensible. The next 8 bars could be contrasting, possibly in a minor key. This would probably sound less resolute; perhaps sad and discouraged. A musical ear would notice this without any knowledge of harmony itself. Then the last 8 bars could be a repeat of the first 8, back to the major key, giving the impression of a person who, in spite of adversity, carries on, heroic, courageous, determined, noble.

However, to show that it is not quite that simple, here is a little tune from the *William Tell Overture*, with the middle area in the minor key, and the first and last 8 bars in the major key. The general effect is — in some interpretations — almost witty!

In F major

In D minor

Back into F major

In counterpoint, an interesting point emerges. Many of Bach's compositions, even in the very easy Anna Magdalena book, have examples of double counterpoint. This means that the two tunes sound well not only when played as written but also when they are turned upside down! For instance, if the young student is playing the regular piece, you, the parent, can be playing the bass part three or four octaves above — toward the top of the piano if you can manage it. You will find that this sounds very attractive and gives a whole new look to a piece that may have become humdrum through incessant work. That is one reason so many people are devotees of Bach and explains why musicians frequently choose Bach as a vehicle when making arrangements.

The Importance of the Bass Line

Something else that "adds to your listening pleasure" is the ascending or descending bass. In the simpler types of marching band music we become accustomed to a bass that relentlessly consists of C, F, G and C repeated ad nauseam. If you have heard the *Tubby the Tuba* record, you will know what I mean. Country and Western music is full of those basic root notes.

There is nothing wrong with that format but a more effective bass moves step-wise, providing an extra melodic interest. This treatment gives a beef, iron and wine strength to a composition and often adds a certain nobility. A reasonably well-known example is the "Chanson Triste" of Tchaikovsky. Right from the opening bar the bass descends steadily down the scale for ten notes, from B flat to a low G.

Public interest in *The Entertainer* by Scott Joplin, featured in the motion picture *The Sting*, was heightened by the descending bass line in the last few bars of the first section:

It gives a wry strength to what would otherwise be a common-place ending.

All composers use this device. In an article on Cole Porter in the *Saturday Review* of December 25, 1971, Leo Smit commented that Porter absorbed an idea "of great potential and utility from J. S. Bach and other Baroque composers." It was "the descending, chromatic, *lamentoso* bass, over which Christ suffered and Dido wept. Porter carries off his own spectacular ten-note descent in one of his best songs, 'Just One of Those Things'."*

Leo Smit also points out the remarkable similarity of Porter's *Night and Day* with Schumann's *Lotus Flower*. Both have the same chromatic descent but this time it is in the melody. Of course, Cole Porter's studies included time at the Harvard School of Music and the École Normale in Paris. He was quite familiar with the standard effective techniques in musical compositions. To this, he added his own rare and unusually elegant musical gifts.

The Deceptive Cadence

Another device used by all composers is the Deceptive Cadence.

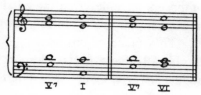

V to I is the normal
     perfect cadence.
V7 to VI is the deceptive
     cadence mentioned above.

That is an idiom used by organists who must ensure that the last strains of the wedding music come just as the bride reaches the altar. If he sees the need to lengthen the composition, the deceptive cadence offers an excellent solution.

The comedy team of Nicols and May used that device in an amusing skit where Elaine May played the part of the president of the local P.T.A. The pianist was to open the meeting with the national anthem but kept, by mistake, going into deceptive cadences over and over. Finally Elaine May said, icily, "Stop playing!" The same device is used by Dudley Moore in his brilliant parody of the Colonel Bogie March in the comedy review, *Good Evening Friends*.

Use Modern Influences to Advantage

It is because of this present-day link between what we used to call serious or classical music and Broadway show music, that I urge parents to give their children the best of both worlds. The record albums of effectively constructed rock or popular music can be invaluable in increasing the interest of piano students. Certain rock or pop artists are particularly creative in this area — Emerson, Lake and Palmer, Chuck Mangione, Rick Wakeman, and the Japanese arranger, Tomita, are only a few examples.

Those who are developing this broad background will also find much of interest in modern serious music including electronic music and some using the Moog synthesizer. Professor John Weinzweig, a well-known Canadian composer, recently commented on why modern composers have deserted the tried and true paths of the older composers, and are exploring new and exciting concepts. He says, "The music of our society is reflected in the new music of today. In all other aspects of human activity, including the visual and literary arts, we are very much concerned with the present. It is utterly illogical that in music we should dwell almost entirely in the past. Must contemporary music await the excavations of some future musical archeologist? The composer needs his public now: — sorry, he cannot wait." You as parents can help develop this public.

Besides western music there is always other music to be explored. Indian music, for instance, which seems odd to our ears at first is also divided into both classical and popular. It should be noted than an exponent of Indian music, such as Ravi Shankar, plays differently here on this continent than when he is in India. Japanese and African music, as well as the folk music of Western Europe, is also worth investigation for anyone interested in unusual patterns of construction.

11

MEANING

Once students have developed some technique, a control of tone colour, an ability to decide on tempi and a knowledge of construction, what do they do with it? One of the exciting things about music is expressing one's own ideas arrived at, I admit, often after a bit of nudging and hinting by the teacher in the early years. Since education is a process by which students are transformed into persons who teach themselves, the teacher encourages every evidence of personality that shows through in the student's playing. Even as early as Grade 1, children can be expressing themselves through the piano and the value of this cannot be overemphasized.

A knowledge of keyboard harmony is a necessity. To play along with no idea as to what key one is in, is the same thing as telling a joke in French without knowing the language. It is impossible to put across the punch line. Rattling off music with no idea as to where it is going is as pointless as looking at a stained glass window from the wrong side.

Phrasing in Music

Most of us have noticed that some piano players who have had very little formal training still play more acceptably than others who have been studying for years. Indeed, on one occasion, I heard such a pianist referred to as a person who could "make the piano talk". That phrase interested me and, over the years, its significance has increased. It suggests the idea of phrasing which is the same in music as in speech.

Take the phrase, "Woe is Me". I have learned that if an actor wanted to say that phrase with the utmost eloquence, he would, first of all, take a deep breath and say the word, "Woe" with conviction, then ride the vowel, "O" with considerable resonance. He would then join the last two words, "is Me", to this. For the last word, however, he would be supposedly almost out of breath with emotion and so he would say the "Me" softly and possibly make it a little bit shorter. To imitate this on the piano, one comes down from above with arm weight on the first note with a rich tone. Then this sound is transferred to the next note — very well joined — and finally the last note is played softly and shorter, to indicate exhaustion.

Phrasing in music is indicated by a slur over the notes. Since the phrasing is marked carelessly in poorly edited music, once again it is wise to buy music published by well-known and respected firms. If there is a question of whether to observe a phrase or not, it is a good idea to *sing* the passage and do what comes naturally. If, in singing, it sounds quite wrong to clip off the supposed phrase, do not do it.

Another example to illustrate this same point is the phrase, "Oh Dear!" There again one can imagine taking in a huge breath before starting. Consequently the, "Oh" will be rich and resonant. The *Dear*, on the other hand, when the actor is *out* of breath, will be soft and dropped off with the last remnants of breath. Both these examples are indicated in musical notation below:

74

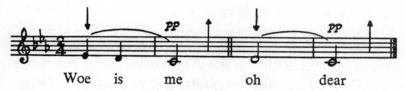

Woe   is   me   oh   dear

Another element of phrasing has to do with the way a note diminishes in intensity. If one note of a legato passage is an extremely long one, it is wise to adjust the following note, matching it to the previous note's intensity at that moment. (The first note will have died somewhat.)

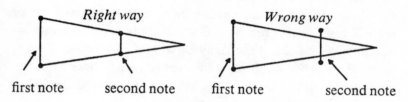

All of these comments arise naturally when one approaches the piano as an instrument comparable to the human voice. As Casals, the famous cellist, said, "The printed page is inadequate. It is our privilege to breath life into it!"

Sequences

Before a performance can be considered, a composition must have been learned so well that it gives the impression of being improvised, or freshly minted. The student should be taught to look for sequences. A sequence is a passage that is repeated at a higher or lower pitch more or less identically. Here is an example:

I mentioned earlier that a piece must always "go somewhere" and sequences are a good way of suggesting direction. They add intensity. They can be likened to a mother calling her child. She calls once. No answer. She calls again, obviously a little louder. And so on. Sequences must always be observed but the pianist can decide whether it is to be a rising one or descending one. The intensity must always increase or decrease and never stay constant. Otherwise one creates a tiresome fence of equally stressed notes.

Searching for New Ideas

In breathing life into a number, the student is like an actor who searches out particularly meaningful lines to be stressed. He or she will learn to experiment to find unusually effectives notes — one note of the chord that may be of special interest. That is where the teacher will bring added experience to bear with suggestions. Chapter 10 contains comments that could profitably be considered in this regard.

Paderewski was a pianist who excelled at finding these nuggets — notes of particular beauty to bring out. He said, "Take time to be beautiful," and many of our best pianists delight us with the new insights that they provide when they play familiar numbers. The important thing is that students must recreate the piece every time they play it for anyone. They will have, perhaps, played it one hundred times but in only *one* performance, they must bring the whole composition fully to life for their listener.

A father took his little child to a circus and she was very much impressed with one of the clowns. On the way out, they happened to pass close to this clown and so the father introduced his little daughter. The clown responded by shaking hands with the child, whereupon the youngster exclaimed, "Why, there's a people in there!" That is what must constantly be recaptured in piano playing — the sense of a "real person in there". A Grade One piece with meaning is much more enjoyable than a Grade Ten without it.

Some years ago, at the Winnipeg Festival, I heard a number of Grade One choirs. One little group caught my attention particularly as there was something forlorn about them. For one thing, they weren't an example of "spit and polish" as were some of their competitors with their neatly-pressed outfits. Also, they represented almost every ethnic group. Their teacher, with her back to the audience, was putting in the time while they were awaiting the adjudicator's bell to start their singing. During this period they were standing at ease, looking like youngsters anywhere, neither sad nor gay. When the bell rang, the teacher motioned to them and they huddled more closely together with all eyes on her face. Then for a moment, she must have been telling them something of significance because their faces gradually assumed quite a solemn air preparatory to telling us their story.

They had chosen to sing "Little Bo-Peep" in a simple little arrangement suiting the Grade One level. However, their voices were so pure and they sang with such conviction that they had everyone's attention. As the song continued, the facial expression of these little mites became more and more serious until, when they came to the line, "And they'd left their tails behind them", many of us found that our eyes were filled with tears. We were not the only ones affected. Sir Hugh Roberton, one of the most famous of Scottish adjudicators, said he had never heard more moving singing. He gave them the remarkable mark of 96!

12

SIGHT READING

One of the most chilling experiences a musician can have is to be confronted with a new piece of music, possibly an accompaniment, in public, and told to read it right off the bat. I still remember with horror such situations. People who haven't tried hardly realize how difficult it is to handle an accompaniment at sight. Few experienced pianists, on the other hand, think that they themselves are good at sight reading. The trouble is that as skill increases, so do our standards.

I had one adult student who was an exception to this rule. When she first began to study with me, she was so confident of her reading ability that she would, literally, tackle anything. Unfortunately, she had had little training and was unaware of what a mediocre job she was doing. Because she was a very gifted person, over our years together she completely revamped her playing and came to enjoy going into things in depth. She laughingly told me that when she came to me she could read *anything* whereas when she concluded her studies with me, she could play *nothing*!

The Uses of Sight Reading

Some years ago one of the leading American Glee Clubs held auditions across the country for positions that required first-rate sight reading. They needed people who could read so well that only one rehearsal would be necessary for their various television and radio appearances. It was found that only seventeen out of one thousand came up to the required standard in spite of the fact that most of the applicants were seasoned professionals who had been trained in various music schools.

Skill in sight reading is valuable because it opens up all kinds of delightful possibilities for work with friends and colleagues. The simplest example is the fun of playing nursery tunes for youngsters to clap, dance and sing to. A good sight reader is always in demand as a Grade One or Kindergarten teacher. But that is only a start. Playing accompaniments for friends who sing is a never-ending source of pleasure, as is the experience of playing duets.

Chamber music, playing with other instruments, is fascinating. At an elementary level many instruction books for string instruments and woodwinds provide piano accompaniments that can be read at sight by those who have developed some competence in this rewarding area.

Much more demanding material is contained in the magnificent sonatas, trios and quintets by Schubert, Beethoven, Brahms, Schumann — to name only a few. Even excellent sight readers rarely play these works without perfecting them first. Works for voice and piano ("lieder") and sonatas for violin and piano are considered to be duets and so are worked out with care by both musicians. But, although meticulous preliminary work is essential for a public performance, many gifted sight readers play such numbers with each other for recreation and inspiration.

79

Admitting at the outset that sight reading is not easy, I hasten to add that it is easier to gain some competence than it was when music was harder to come by. If the problem is attacked head on, it is amazing what results can be obtained by even ten minutes a day spent on this work.

Setting Up a Sight Reading Program

Teresa Carreno's father made her practise sight reading for ten minutes a day, no more, no less, when she was a tot. "And what was the result?" said the great pianist fifty years later. "By the time I was fourteen, I could read anything, absolutely anything, at sight!"

Students learning to read music are best served by reading *music*, not by drill on material which has no musical meaning. You see, it is not enough to be able to figure out a melody and play it on the piano. Students must be able to hear the tune in their head before playing it. We all know how surprised we would be to see someone reading a book by sounding all the words. No literate person needs to. They know that they can get the message by glancing over the page silently. And so, in music, students need to recognize the music of a familiar tune without having to play it. That is why it is necessary to supplement the actual sight reading practice with ear training. There are many excellent ear training texts on the market and most teachers will have their favorites.

Sight reading cannot begin too early. For instance, let us suppose that the child has been studying for from three to six months. At this point, the student can, perhaps, figure out the notes from music to piano and do simple counting. The time at lessons is so limited that encouragement with sight-reading by the parent at home is a helpful supplement. It does not need to be unduly time-consuming. To be palatable, sight work must be easy — so easy that the child thinks, "This is a cinch!" and gets pleasure from the ability to play it. After students have had six months of study, the teacher will probably give them the easiest book she or he can find, and get them to try playing the pieces. When a point of resistance is reached, another easy book can be begun and continued until problems are encountered; then another book, and so on. This allows the youngster to become familiar with different printing, type setting and the like. That period will be a rewarding one for the child if there is feedback from the parents. Encouragement at home means that much can be accomplished with little lesson time being consumed. Inevitably the point at which resistance appears will be further and further along and I can assure you that a surprising facility can be developed. In the meantime, the student is making normal progress with the regular work. When a number of students pursue this plan, they often share the books with one another.

The Secret of Success — A Hymn Book

After some competence has been reached in reading in the early grades, a real breakthrough can be made by starting to use a hymn book as a text. It had never occurred to me that a hymn book could be useful until I met a young man who played popular music with great facility and inventiveness. He was said to have never had a lesson but later, in conversation with me, he admitted that he *had* had lessons. However, he said that he had learned best by using the organ in the chapel of the private school he attended.

He spent hours browsing through a hymn book and got more ideas from it than from the lessons he was taking. You may wonder what hymn book has this special magic. You will find that there is a remarkable similarity between most denominational hymn books. Many lovely hymns by composers like Bach, Mendelssohn and Haydn, have been used by all. In most cases respected musicians, regardless of their religious leanings, were engaged as musical consultants to aid in compiling these books. So almost any hymn book that contains four-part harmony and good clear type can be used. Such books are readily available through church offices or through music stores.

The student may start with the simplest hymns, those with no sharps or flats, seeing how many chords can be read in the space of one minute and paying no attention to the time signature or to giving each chord its right "count". The object is to improve the speed in reading four-part harmony. Students may set up graphs and register on them just how many chords are read in each session of one minute. At first the students may read as few as four or five chords in that time. There will be surprisingly wide variations. Indeed, the graph will look like a very active stock market chart, moving up and down. Each student, of course, will fill in his or her graph at home and may occasionally bring it to the lessons if the teacher so desires. Many students find this quite fascinating and yet the valuable lesson time is available for other facets of the work. It is only worthwhile, however, if at least ten trials are done each day. Many students do many more than that once they become interested and see that their scores are taking off.

For example: a child may breeze in from school and call to Mother, "Look at the clock and tell me when to start". That is the signal for the parent to say, "Ready, set, go!" and "stop!" when the exact minute is over. That can easily be done if the kitchen has a large clock or the mother has a watch. It should not unduly upset the preparation of meals. In fact such a game contributes to a warm relationship and is fun! This kind of exercise takes none of the time that the teacher needs for more pressing matters and yet progress can be remarkable. I have seen students who started with a figure of between five and ten chords per minute work up to one hundred a minute! If inaccuracies creep in, start deducting five seconds for every error.

As soon as feasible, the student should analyze the easier chords and older students, with large hands, can try expanding those chords. This is done by playing the bass in octaves, doubling the melody with the right hand and filling in, still with the right hand, the other notes of the chord. This is excellent for gaining a knowledge of harmony and facility in playing four-note chords.

Later, a student might enjoy making up a descant for a simple hymn. Great fun! Then the family can sing it while the student plays the regular hymn. Home-grown music has a special flavour!

Adding Other Material

In the meantime, of course, the reading of other material than hymns continues and, if the student does sight work *in addition* to usual practice, as a kind of recreation, the results will be extraordinary. I mentioned earlier that there is nearly always an initial resistance to sight work and the parent is wise to show enthusiasm and persistence in seeing that it is done. However, if the first material is extremely easy and lots of encouragement is given, sight reading becomes a self-propelling interest.

Two things are important: First, students must learn to ignore mistakes and get on with it. (Professional musicians admit that a good sight reader must know instantly what he can leave out.) Second, to counteract any tendency toward sloppiness, the teacher may take a hand and suggest that some of this easier material be prepared with a very high standard of precision.

If the parent can play, even a small amount, the interest in sight work can be a delight. There are some excellent duet books available that are written for teacher and student and, if the parent can play the teacher part, it is most rewarding. Some references to these may be found in Chapter 6.

Learning Rhythmic Patterns

One difficulty that arises in sight reading is getting the rhythmic pattern right from the start, and enunciating it clearly. Each piece consists of a series of notes of different values fitted into the framework of the beat. We can walk in time and can soon sing rhythmically complicated tunes against our own walking. But these we would, of course, be unable to write down. Translating rhythmic patterns from the printed page of music is quite another matter. Here, knowing the *French time names* is invaluable. They were invented by a French lawyer at the turn of the last century. The system is a simple one and in it the rhythm is expressed by syllables rather than mathematical terms. For instance, as a start, one calls the unit (the denominator of the time signature) 'Tah'.

So, in 3/4 time we have ♩ ♩ ♩ Tah Tah Tah. A half note is expressed by 'Tah—ah.' ♩

So, in 3/4 time we have ♩   ♩ Tah-ah Tah. Thus a dotted half note would be ♩. Tah-ah-ah. Proceeding to faster notes 2 running eighth notes ♫ would be TaTé. When a note is tied the consonant 'T' is not sounded as in:

♩ ♫ ♩ Tah taté Tah

♩ ♫ ♩ Tah até Tah

A triplet is expressed as Tatéti- something like the word merrily.

♪♪♪ (3)

Four sixteenths is expressed as tafatifi.

84

tah ta fa ti fi tah tah   tah tah tah–ah

One of the most helpful syllabic patterns in the whole system is the dotted eighth followed by a sixteenth: ♩. ♪ That usually presents problems to the student but in this system it is expressed as: ♩. ♪ ta-fi. The folk tune *Country Gardens* comes to mind as an example of this:

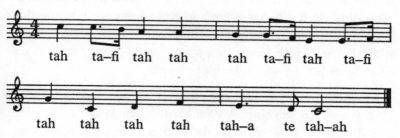

tah ta–fi tah tah   tah ta–fi tah ta–fi

tah tah tah tah   tah–a te tah–ah

Teachers may question the use of the French time names in simple passages where ordinary methods of counting would work as well. They are quite right. Nonetheless, it is a useful supplement in areas that defy ordinary methods, like Country Gardens — shown above. It is best to use the parts that fit best into the overall plan. It helps students to grasp, not just single notes, but whole rhythmical groups at a glance. Once these are mastered one of the chief stumbling blocks to good sight work has been removed.

Winning the War Against Staleness

One of the reasons that skill in sight reading is so essential is that it eliminates boredom, a state that must be avoided at all costs. It is so easy to become stale. Franz Aller, whose orchestra played for *My Fair Lady* during its long-term run in New York, found boredom was his worst problem. After having played the score many thousands of times his players tended to relax and play in a perfunctory manner. He was acutely aware of the fact that, if someone from a distance came to New York to see and hear the show, he should find it fresh as paint. To combat this ennui, he arranged for his orchestra, at rehearsal, to play all kinds of string quartets and chamber music in order to enliven their work and renew the thrill that comes from a new experience. He also went to the trouble of having the score rearranged in many ways. Each night a different player would find that *he* had the melody or counter melody. A constant new look! Concentrating on the old score would have been so tiresome that the musicians would have actually dreaded each performance. With the freshened score each player could hardly wait to see what "goodies" he would be given to play.

Learning to play certain set pieces is only one part of music. That is why, in learning to sight-read, students should use the widest possible variety of music. Playing the same thing over and over can be deadly. A cellist of my acquaintance tells of dreaming that he was in an orchestra playing the Elgar *Enigma Variations*. He woke up and found he was!

13

CONCLUDING NOTES

And now, good luck! Do keep in mind that playing the piano is an enterprise that will bring a certain radiance to your family's time together. If you have done nothing up to the present to forge a link with music, do not despair. Start as of now! There will always be a gap between what one could have done and what one has done.

Be easy-going about it. Try to maintain a relaxed emotional climate. Your own musical enthusiasm is your principal asset. If it is strong and constant, it will be contagious.

Two earlier points are worth repeating: one is that it is great to know how to attack a problem and solve it; the other is that adversity can be used to advantage by the parent to show that the family is strongly behind the child, win or lose. These two points lead to a strong sense of security and confidence that help students when, later, they are presented with any challenging situation.

An Irreversible Urge

We often hear the comment that musicians are jealous of one another. I have found that that is not true. Indeed, one of my greatest pleasures has been in playing two-piano works with other musicians and playing with chamber music groups. That is why I hope that your children will have such an irreversible urge toward music that, no matter where they may be in later life, they will seek out and have a part in the musical experience of the community. In urban centres they would probably defer to the leadership of someone more highly qualified. In small towns, they might have to assume leadership themselves.

I am not forgetting that such an objective is only achieved through hard work. But having a sense of humour and being responsive to fun is a determining factor in making the work-time fly by. A student told me that "if you want to play like an angel, you must practise like the devil!"

Parents try to keep abreast of the latest ideas regarding diet and nutrition. Television does not allow us to forget the necessity of good grooming. What is not as fully presented is the desirability of food for the spirit. George Eliot believed that music, art and literature offer a means of expanding mental and emotional horizons and thus of making one more responsive to every nuance of life. She has one of her characters say, "Certain strains of music affect me so strangely, — I can never hear them without their changing my whole attitude of mind for a time and, if the effect would last, I might be capable of heroisms."

The value of music in developing this heroism or sense of responsibility came very much to mind recently when I adjudicated a rhythm band of Junior Kindergarten age. Some of these children were from underprivileged areas and, in one case, included some tiny children who had only been in this country for a few weeks. It would be hard to exaggerate the value of this participation to the little ones involved. They looked so proud

88

and responsible, watching with the greatest care for their time to come in with their instruments. These small newcomers were also learning some of the music of their adopted country and surely it is as important to know a country's music, "as it is to know the number of pounds of bacon exported or the number of towns with over 10,000 population!"*

It is our privilege to put out a hand to welcome children into the adult world. We must not make them earn our acceptance. We should avoid being so critical of technical shortcomings that we miss what they are trying to express. Encouragement is like the sun: it causes personalities to become radiant, warm and glowing. The technique will come.

In a recent interview, the originator of *Sesame Street* said that had she the chance to do it again, she would completely change the basic setup. Instead of concentrating on getting letters and numbers across to the children, she would have stressed things like courtesy and safety. She continued that she would have been sure that the numbers and letters would be learned at a later date but that the children might never *ever* learn about courtesy and safety. The same is true of music. We all know that the notes and time must be taught at a reasonably early stage but what is more important is the awakening of a lively mind to an awareness of tunes, of exciting rhythms and variations in timbre, not only in orchestral instruments, but in the sounds of nature too.

As parents, we have a vision of what we want for our children. Our concept should be both idealistic and realistic. I hope that my book will give inspiration and encouragement to those of you who are trying to solve some of the most bewildering problems — those of parents.

*Lois Birkenshaw, *Music for Fun, Music for Learning* (Toronto: Holt, Rinehart, Winston, 1974).